Legends and Lore of Lake Ontario

Susan Peterson Gateley

The History Press

Published by The History Press
Charleston, SC 29403
www.historypress.net

Front cover, bottom: courtesy of Jaime C. Jordan (jcjordan@swcp.com).

First published 2013

Manufactured in the United States

ISBN 978.1.62619.084.9

Library of Congress CIP data applied for.

Notice: The information in this book is true and complete to the best of our knowledge. It is offered without guarantee on the part of the author or The History Press. The author and The History Press disclaim all liability in connection with the use of this book.

CONTENTS

ACKNOWLEDGEMENTS

I would like to thank the following history-minded folk who made this book possible:

Ed Moriarity for sharing his story of an Oswego "shipwreck."

Richard Palmer and his tireless excavation of old news archives and other primary source documentation of our past.

Walter Lewis for his excellent website resources at www.maritimehistoryofthegreatlakes.ca.

Dale Austin, Ed Burtt, June MacArthur, Wade Szilagyi, Greg Grunditsch and Brenda Spencer, who made available some wonderful and, in some cases, priceless images from family archives for this project.

Pat Cooper for her generosity regarding her artwork.

The artists of Red Creek School District, Jamie Kiemle and Katie Dawson, and their instructor, Sue Stanistreet—many thanks for your efforts.

And the tireless technical department in the form of Chris Gateley.

CHAPTER 1

GHOSTS IN THE NIGHT

What is it about a good ghost story that we find so compelling? Even most disbelievers enjoy a tale told by candlelight or a flickering fire with dark shadows in the corners or jumping and shivering on the walls. Lake Ontario's waters have closed over many vessels, large and small. There have been appalling (and violent) tragedies played out on its shores. We should not be surprised that our region has its share of restless spirits.

Several writers have told of a Lake Ontario demon known as the Carcagne. One of the best-known stories was that told by Samuel Hopkins Adams in his *Grandfather Tales* and adapted here. Female sea devils and spirits abound in the folklore of sailors around the world. Lake Ontario's Carcagne closely resembles the night-flying banshees of Celtic tales with a dash of African-Caribbean jumbie and a bit of Iroquois *Jijogweh*, the night-flying water witch gull. Perhaps Irish immigrants brought their banshee stories to Lake Ontario's shores, where they were cross-pollinated with a black slave story or an Indian legend.

Lake Ontario's devil spirit, the Carcagne, ventures forth on stormy nights to soar over the waves. She has the head of a wolf, a vampire's fangs and the black wings of a bat. One late August night in 1829, a powerful northeaster came sweeping across the water. That night, broken clouds scudded before the gale, and an eerie glow from the Aurora Borealis pulsed, flashed and shimmered to the north. Despite the date, there was an autumn chill in the wind as it rushed among the buildings and swirled down the streets of the port of Oswego. As the breakers boomed against the shore beneath Fort

Ontario, word went around the waterfront taverns that Munk Birgo was putting out onto the lake with his sloop. Birgo was a man with a reputation to match that of the lake banshee. He was born in the malaria-ridden swamps of Montezuma, a day's ride southwest of Oswego, and his mother was said to possess dark powers of her own. Birgo practiced a number of unsavory trades on the lake, including the transport of illegally obtained cadavers for the medical colleges in New York City and Albany, where the "resurrectioners" could get up to fifty dollars for a cadaver in prime condition. Birgo sometimes brought his sloop into Oswego to transfer bodies to a canalboat there.

A small group of waterfront idlers gathered to watch him cast off. Some thought they heard the flutter of wings on the air. Some said they caught the faint odor of corruption. Was it the leech of Birgo's jib they heard and the lingering odor of his sloop's fish hold they smelled? Or were they something more? Munk Birgo cast off that night at the stroke of midnight, 'tis said. He sailed out of the river directly into the northeaster while reciting the Lord's Prayer backward.

The dockside loafers turned and hurried for home. Some said later they heard a high, mad wailing in the night. Perhaps the sound came from the gale whining among the chimney pots and shrilling through the rigging of the ships in port. But perhaps it did not. At dawn the next day, Birgo's black-hulled sloop was seen coming back into port. She was under full sail, and some who saw her declared a small dark cloud or shape moved just ahead of her across the water. She steered straight up the river on a run, moving faster than any mortal sloop could sail. At the helm sat Munk Birgo's bones picked clean and white by the Carcagne. Then, they say, the sloop abruptly vanished, and a wild cry sounded over the harbor.

Oswego is home to another ghost, one of the best known on the New York lakeshore. This phantom is the spirit of a soldier who walks the ramparts of Oswego's Fort Ontario. He is said to appear just before our nation goes to war. This spirit is supposed to have been the restless remains of Lieutenant Basil Dunbar, who was stationed at the fort's predecessor during the French and Indian War and who committed a serious tactical blunder by falling in love with his commanding officer's wife. When the captain found out, a duel was declared, and Dunbar lost. It was not long after that reports of a ghost pacing the fort's ramparts began.

Another version of the Oswego military ghost holds that the spirit that haunts Fort Ontario was that of a British regular who died in Revolutionary War times. He is seen in his red coat and white britches and is said to be the uneasy spirit of George Fykes. He appears at least once to every new garrison

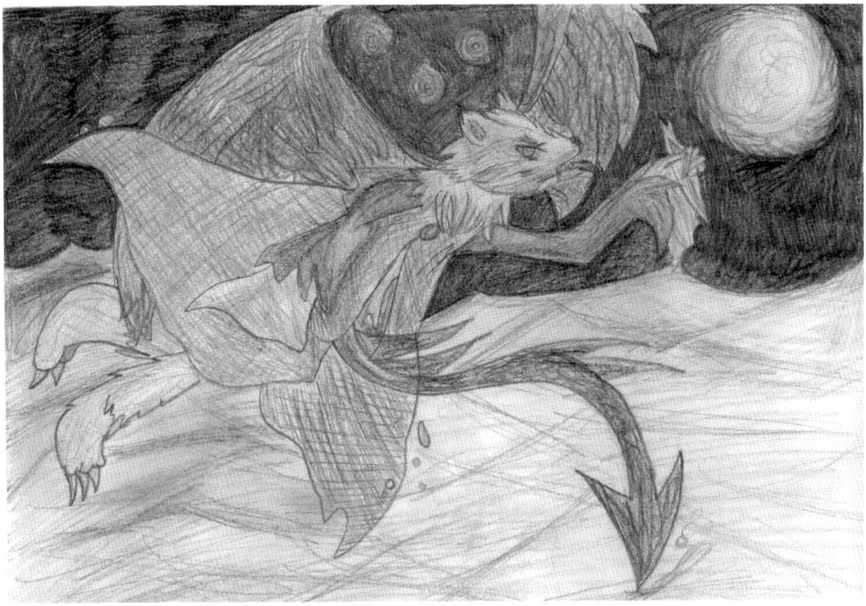

The Carcagne, Lake Ontario's version of the Irish banshee or the night-flying jumbie. *Art by Jamie Kiemle.*

at the fort. Because it is no longer an active military post, it's not surprising that he has not been reported since World War II. But during World War I, a soldier stationed at the fort claimed to have seen an apparition. This was around 1919, and as the rumors spread, the general hysteria became so intense that no one wanted to stand post at this particular station. It all started when a guard noticed a light the size of a saucer following him as he walked along. Thinking it some sort of trick, he ignored it. But the next night, another guard saw the same thing behind him. The two men compared notes. One then watched the other walk his post. At midnight, as city hall struck twelve, the light arrived for duty. This time it stationed itself over the sentry's head and followed him around.

Things got into such a state that a couple men were court-martialed for desertion of duty. At the trial, no fewer than nine witnesses testified that they, too, had seen an unearthly light, like that of a lantern floating in the air. The private on trial was acquitted, probably the only time in military history a deserter was let off by reason of a ghost.

Not to be outdone, Fort Niagara also claims a phantom soldier. He also dates back to the French and Indian War. In 1759, the war was going badly

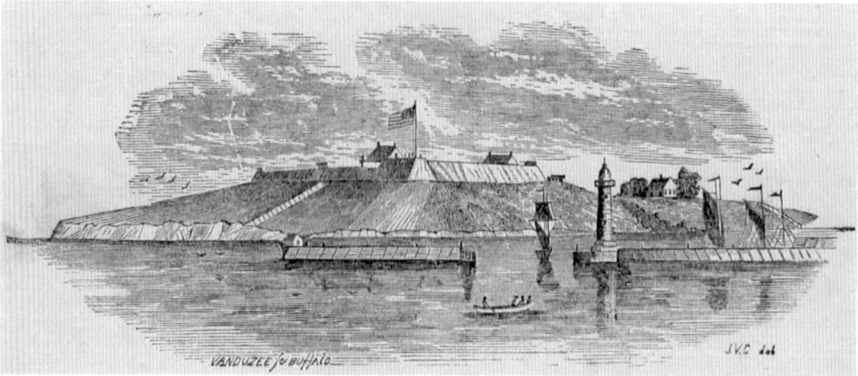

Fort Ontario around the time of the Civil War. *Engraving from a sketch by Van Cleve.*

for the French on Lake Ontario. Frontenac (Kingston) had fallen, cutting Niagara off from any supply lines. Then Sir William Johnson assaulted Niagara with a large force and besieged it. For those inside facing starvation and death from an enemy shell, it was a nerve-wracking time to say the least. Life was bad and getting worse.

It was under these harsh circumstances that two French officers in love with the same Indian maiden decided to settle the affair once and for all with their sabers. As steel clashed and clanged, it was clear that one duelist was outclassed. Then, with a thud, a sword blade cut through flesh and bone, and a head fell on the cobbled courtyard. The luckless lover's body rolled into a well beside the dueling ground. Since then, it's said, the headless soldier sometimes appears on moonlit nights, pacing about the courtyard and searching for his lost body part.

Headless ghosts have long been a part of New York mythology. The headless horseman of Sleepy Hollow still shows up in our area regularly at Fair Haven's annual witches' parade. Usually, such mutilated spirits are unwelcome at best and downright scary at worst. However, not all ghosts are evil. There are stories of ghosts that come back to do the living a good turn of one sort or another. Horace Beck, in *Folklore and the Sea*, describes a drowned fisherman coming aboard as a ghost to help the shorthanded crew of a schooner get its ship through a storm. And Louis C. Jones, in his book *Things That Go Bump in the Night*, even tells of an old horse that rose from its grave to help its master do one last spring plowing. There is also another tale in Jones's book of a helpful ghost from which this story of Samuel Guthrie's return is adapted.

Samuel Guthrie's wood frame house stands square in the middle of Sackets Harbor, a block or two from the shores of Black River Bay. Today, the house is used as a visitors' center, but some years back, it was still a private home. Guthrie was a military doctor stationed at the post who pioneered the use of chloroform in performing surgery. We can assume from this tale that he was also a doctor with a well-developed sense of compassion.

Shortly after the family moved into the one-time physician's home and office, they heard bones rattle in the room where Guthrie had once kept his skeletons. There were also other occasional manifestations of a ghostly presence, though no one ever saw the doctor as he paced the floor while deep in thought. Then, one evening, there came a need for his services, and true to his calling, he returned from the other world to render a last act of mercy. On that night, the patriarch of the household lay dying. His wife stayed by the old man's bedside to do what she could to ease his passing. As the night dragged on into the small, still hours of morning, the dying man drifted into a coma, and his breathing became shallow, rapid and labored. Gazing on his pale features as he struggled to draw air into his lungs, his wife thought surely his time had come. If only he could pass now, it would be a blessing.

Then she sensed she was no longer alone. She looked to the side, and there by the bed stood a white-haired man wearing a jacket of old-fashioned cut. She recognized him as Dr. Guthrie, for she had seen photos of the house's builder in similar attire. The sudden appearance of what could only be a ghost was such a profound shock that she let out a shriek and fainted. This brought other members of the family to investigate. They found her lying on the floor, and they found their grandfather still and lifeless, at peace at last in his bed. And though there had never been any trace of the chemical in the family's medicine cabinet, the room was permeated by the heavy, distinctive odor of chloroform.

In 1945, Walter Henry Green published *Great Sodus Bay History, Reminiscences Anecdotes and Legends*, copies of which are often available in libraries near Sodus. He recorded several ghost stories from the shores of the bay, two of which follow. One, the ghost of Mink Creek, tells of the aftermath of a murder.

According to this tale, on moonlit nights, a man was often seen crouching by the little stream and washing his hands. At least once, a witness approached the apparition and spoke to it, only to see it fade away. A story made the rounds that this was the ghost of an early squatter who came to the area and was attracted to the land by the lake. He claimed the forest on both sides of the creek's outlet and built a rude hut there. He lived by selling furs and odds and ends of food, such as the mushrooms, herbs and blackberries he found in the forest. He had never bothered to put a claim on the land and had saved nearly enough money to pay for it when a family of settlers appeared on the opposite shore of "his" creek.

The lonely recluse loved the dark hemlocks, the tall oaks and the clear running stream that slipped into the lake just east of a high bluff, and he was determined to have his land. He watched the settlers as they made camp at the site of their planned cabin. Then, after all were asleep, he crept into the camp and silently drove his sharp long knife into the heart of one after another of the luckless family. He murdered them all—man, wife and two children. Afterward, his hands red with blood, he fled. A little way from the camp, he stopped to wash his hands in the creek. Then, the sudden shot of a rifle rang out, and he toppled dead into its waters to mingle his own fresh blood with what he had just cleansed from his hands.

It seemed that a neighbor youth had been drawn forth from his home by the bright summer moon and had decided to call on his new chum at the settler's camp. He arrived just as the murderer was finishing off the last of the sleeping family members, and he watched him slip away along the bank. Seizing the dead settler's rifle, he followed and performed his own act of frontier justice. He then buried all the dead a short way from the creek and left the scene. He kept the affair a secret, but Green suggests it may explain the mysterious disappearance of Bill Waters, a squatter whom the record shows lived on Salmon Creek in Pultneyville.

Salmon Creek appears to have been a particularly spectral stretch of shore, since there was a farmhouse nearby also said to be haunted. The spirit seen here was that of a child. A boy, sick from pneumonia, lay long ill in his bed. The neighbors, from time to time, took turns relieving his parents by staying for a night to watch and care for the invalid child. One night, the caretaker on watch heard the boy complain that there was something heavy on his chest. The caretaker then saw materialize before him a large pure black cat lying curled on the child's chest. He struck at it, and the cat instantly vanished. The boy was relieved, but all that night, a thunderous sound was heard going around the house. It sounded like a heavy wagon traveling rapidly over rough, frozen ground. A few days later, the child died.

Perhaps that murder by Mink Creek did occur in the area at a time when law enforcement was scant. But there is another theory, recorded by Green, for the origin of the ghostly black cat story. He writes that the haunted house and sick child tale began making the rounds after one of several heirs to the farm tried to buy his siblings out, and no one would sell. Green says he devised the black cat to drive down the price when the estate was put up for auction.

Sometimes, ghosts may not actually show themselves, but signs and omens appear that are difficult to explain as being anything other than spectral in origin. And new ghost stories continue to surface. For example, there is one of a woman in white who occasionally opens a window upstairs at a Fair Haven bed-and-breakfast. The old brick house stands at the mouth of a little stream known locally by the curious name River Styx, the mythological waterway to Hades. This River Styx separated the dry town of Sterling from the wet jurisdiction in Wayne County (also known to locals and teetotalers as the dark side). A short walk from the river stood Joe Deshane's saloon, the Palace, along with another tavern. Here the thirsty folk of Fair Haven were always welcome.

The house ghost is reportedly seen enjoying her rocking chair in one of the upstairs bedrooms or on the stairs dressed in a white robe or nightgown. She opens windows when she feels that some fresh air is in order. There is no theory about her identity or how this restless shade might have come to revisit the old house. Perhaps she has something to do with what happened a long time ago in the basement.

I was told that the family living in the house many years ago once gave shelter to an indigent, broken-down old man who knocked on their door in late fall. Accounts differ as to whether he was a lake sailor, beached by age and infirmity, or a "drummer," as traveling salesmen were known back in the nineteenth century. At any rate, the story goes that the family put him up, giving him a spare bedroom. He died that winter. They couldn't dig a grave when the ground was frozen, so they buried him in the basement. My informant didn't tell me whether he was ever reburied. If the basement is his final resting place, it could explain why the female ghost occasionally visits the house. She could be a restless shade seeking her lost loved one.

Other ghosts also continue to appear around the area. Red Creek has a haunted grocery store. A strange floating globe of light, much like that of Fort Ontario fame, has been seen prowling around the shelves, but only on the side of the building that was once used as a funeral parlor. And not too many years ago, a ghostly presence was reported to haunt the small public park at the north end of Little Sodus Bay known as the West Barrier Bar. The "west side," as the locals call it, is a low-lying, wind-swept gravel spit that separates the bay from the open lake. It has been witness to several tragic drownings over the years and at least one recent suicide.

On November 29, 1868, a small schooner under the command of Captain Thomson loaded lumber in North Fair Haven. Manned by her captain and one sailor, a stranger to the little port, she cast off and set sail on Friday, a day

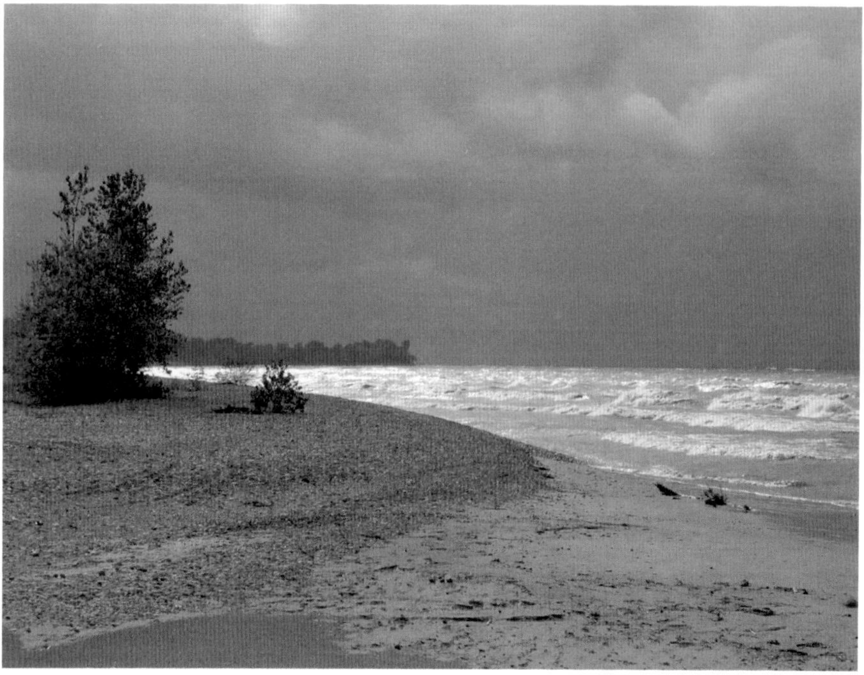

View of the lake from the West Barrier Bar on a squally late summer day. *Author's collection.*

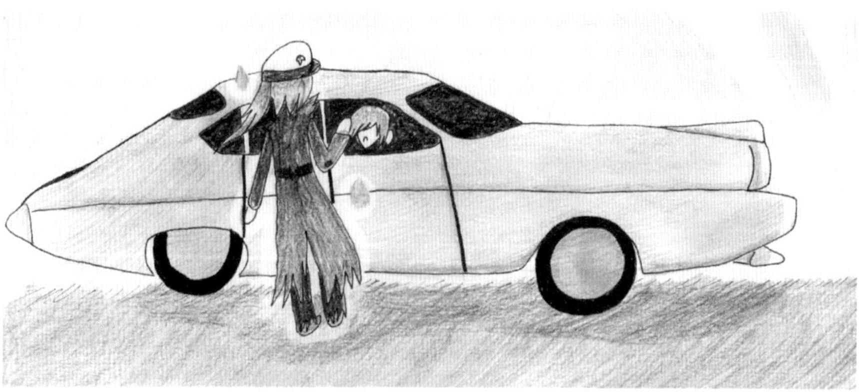

West Barrier Bar ghost. *By Katie Dawson.*

all sailors know to be ill fated for departures. The wind was blowing hard, and the ship soon disappeared into the black night. A few hours later, the sailor who had been hired to work the ship came ashore in the yawl boat. He reported the schooner had suddenly sprung a leak and that, after working the pumps until they were exhausted, they had gotten into the yawl to save themselves. However, the yawl had capsized, and the ship's captain had drowned. The sailor had managed to right the boat and get ashore with her.

The next morning, however, the "sunken" schooner was spotted off Fair Haven still afloat and apparently anchored. Several men went to investigate and found scarcely a bit of bilge water in her pump well. They hurried back ashore, hunted down the strange sailor and had him detained on suspicion of murder. Captain Thomson, it was well known, had $700 on his person. The next day, the captain's body washed ashore at Little Sodus. It was apparent that he had sustained a severe head injury. It was also apparent that his money belt and cash were missing. The strange sailor was at once arrested.

Fast-forward a hundred years or so. One fall evening, a couple teenagers were parked in a car on the west side, watching the sunset over the lake and doing what male and female teens often do in cars in lightly traveled areas. Suddenly, a man appeared on the passenger's side and stared in the window. As the girl recalled, he did not look friendly. Rather, he seemed angry as he scowled into the car. She said he appeared to have a heavy coat and a peaked cap that gave him a nautical appearance. She told me that she thought perhaps he could have been a sea captain. His face was weathered and wrinkled, so he was not young. He also appeared to be soaking wet, which was a bit odd since it wasn't raining.

She was quite frightened by him as he glared at her and turned in alarm to her boyfriend. When she looked back out the window, the man had vanished. Both teenagers got out of the car and looked around, using the boyfriend's flashlight. No trace of the angry man turned up. But the young woman remains convinced she saw a ghost. She asked if I knew of any murders that had ever occurred on the West Barrier Bar. No, I had not heard of any, but there was that old news story of a death just off shore on a late fall night in 1868.

Ghostly apparitions often seem to associate with a physical object or location, such as old houses, nineteenth-century stone fortresses or historic ships. One rarely hears of a haunted office building. Dark, shadowed and maybe a bit musty is more in keeping for the uneasy entities of the spirit world. Nor have I heard of many haunted yachts. Possibly the relationships between pleasure boats and their deceased owners are rarely intense enough to bring ghosts back to their old vessels. But I have heard of a few yachts with supernatural crews. One year, an old wooden cabin cruiser showed up at the Clayton Antique Boat show. Back aft sat a somewhat incongruous rocking chair, the favored spot of a long-departed former owner. The boat's current caretaker claimed that even when the boat had been motionless in calm water at her dock for many hours, the chair would rock, as if the elderly deceased skipper were still enjoying a visit aboard his beloved yacht.

I, too, am associated with an old wooden boat, a gaff-rigged schooner called *Sara B.* She isn't haunted, as far as we know, but she did once give us cause to wonder about the possibility. She looks like a good candidate for harboring a restless shade with her black hull, wooden deadeyes, antique hardware and archaic rig. And at the time, "musty" was a reasonable description of her condition below decks. The first time we sailed on the calm waters of the lake on a gentle early summer morning, we heard a strange, slightly plaintive murmuring from aloft. It sounded like chords softly drawn from a cello's lower register. We gazed skyward pondering the strangely evocative harmonies and wondered whether some far-off trio of old sailors was having a glass together in a celestial tavern and humming a lament for a departed shipmate. "It's the new leather on the gaff jaws breaking in," declared a pragmatic guest. But the boat's two owners, thinking of their yacht's eventful and, at times, troubled past looked at each other and smiled.

A few years before my association with *Sara B*, I heard a haunted boat story from a gentleman tied up at the dock with his fiberglass sloop in Cape Vincent. He was originally from Britain and claimed to be a bit "fey" as he offered this tale of a fellow yachtsman's strange end. There once was a pair of good sailing friends who, with their wives and families, cruised their yachts in company around the lake. One skipper, however, was cheating on his first mate by fooling around with the other's wife. One day, the faithless skipper and his spouse were anchored at Cedar Island in the St. Lawrence near Kingston. They decided to take a stroll around the granite rocks before settling back in the cockpit for happy hour. Alas, the skipper slipped and fell twenty feet, landed on a huge outcrop of rock and died instantly of a broken neck.

Not long after that, his good friend was sailing off Simco Island, alone aboard his own yacht on a warm starlit night, when he saw the deceased skipper step aboard over the life lines. Another time, he encountered his former companion below decks in the galley. And several times, he saw the apparition sitting quietly in the cockpit looking out over the lake. Not until the dead skipper's wife also had a heart attack and passed on did the specter

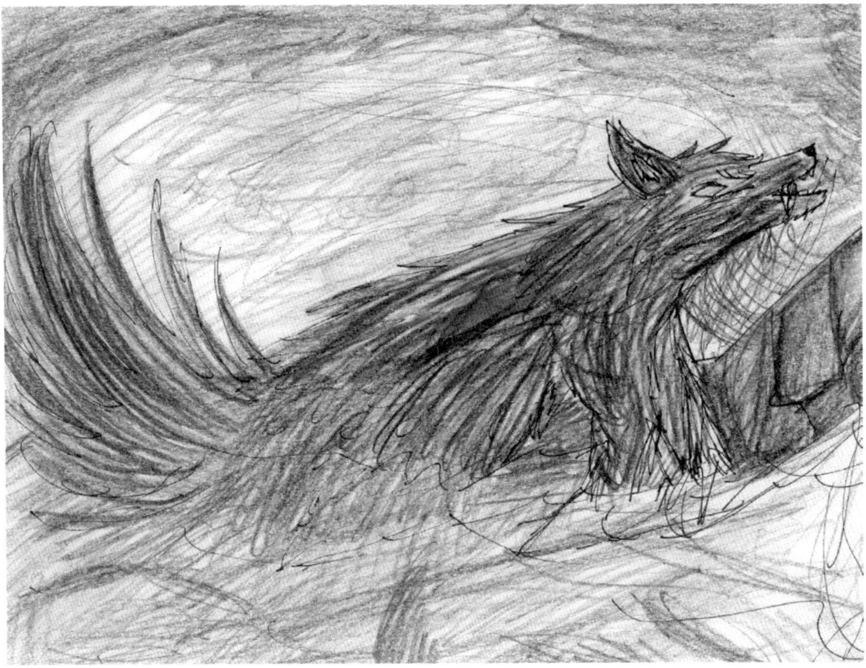

The Black Dog. *By Jamie Kiemle.*

finally stop his night visits. As my informant put it, "He never came back after she died. I guess they're together now."

Lake Ontario even had a ghost dog once, back in the days of sail and steam. C.H.J. Snider wrote of the canine in his "Schooner Days" column published in 1937. The black hellhound appears at night and is associated with death in many areas of the British Isles (the hound of Sherlock Holmes fame being one such spectral animal). Perhaps the black dog legend was transplanted from the United Kingdom to Lake Ontario in this foreshadowing of the death of the schooner *I.G. Jenkins* and her entire crew.

Snider wrote that the stout, strongly built *I.G. Jenkins* was bound down for Oswego from Lake Erie in November 1875 with a cargo of grain when she reached Port Colborne at the entrance to the Welland Canal. Here one of the crew members quit. He followed the ship on the towpath along the canal, refueling at every tavern along the way, the story goes, and always telling the same tale. When he had been at the wheel one calm moonlit night in Lake Erie a few days before, he had seen a large black dog climb up over the rail from the water, walk across the deck "as plain as day," climb the rail on the opposite side and vanish into the lake. The captain had his own pet dog on board, but the sailor insisted that this phantom hound was not the captain's because the captain's dog was still onboard after the ghost dog had vanished over the rail.

To this poor seer, probably a victim of corn juice, the apparition was a warning that the vessel, and all hands aboard, would be lost. So he left when the ship got to Port Colborne. He kept following the *Jenkins* as she towed through the canal, tearfully urging his shipmates to do likewise. The captain finally set his own dog on him to get rid of him.

The *Jenkins* reached Port Dalhousie and towed out at once into Lake Ontario to prevent any further desertions. It came on to blow that night, and the wind veered from southwest to west and northwest. By the next morning, a huge sea was running. Two other schooners also bound for Oswego barely made it into port. A Canadian schooner, the *Delaware*, staggered into Oswego while other ships ran for shelter elsewhere. One vessel reported seeing the *Jenkins* west of Rochester but then lost sight of her when the gale slammed into the fleet, screaming and roaring through their rigging. She never arrived. The *Jenkins* was never seen again.

These days, spirits may have a harder time making themselves heard or seen. They have to compete with such an array of noisy media. TV, iPods, smart phones and the like make it hard to hear anyone rapping on the walls. Perhaps the spirit world thrives in a quieter setting, where people have time to simply sit back and observe their surroundings and can hear the wind in the trees, the cry of a night bird or the howls of distant coyotes outside. Rural electrification and ear buds have made life more difficult for twenty-first-century ghosts.

But I believe folks will repeat tall tales and ghost stories around Lake Ontario for as long as they respect the lake's power. These stories originate from that ageless sense of wonder that lives on among those who follow the water.

CHAPTER 2

MONSTERS, MIRAGES AND OTHER LAKE ONTARIO MYSTERIES

Lake Ontario is big and deep and cold. Its vast dark depths hide many secrets, and over the years, numerous people have told of bizarre events, objects and mysterious life forms residing within them. Some unusual events peculiar to the big lake, such as mirages and seiches, have readily understandable explanations, well grounded in science. Other mysterious occurrences, such as occasional sightings of monsters or the odd rain shower containing fish, frogs and other aquatic organisms, take a bit of unraveling. And some things simply can't be explained.

Very early in my career as a lake watcher, I observed a strange and periodic current that flowed in and out of Pultneyville's small harbor. Often, the water level in the harbor fluctuated just a few inches, but sometimes it would change a foot or more within a few minutes. "It's the tide," the other boaters said. I found the explanation less than satisfying. I'd been a beachcomber for years and had never seen the least evidence of a tide along the open shore. Tides happen on salt water. A bit of research led to the conclusion that a seiche was the cause of the mysterious currents and water level changes. A seiche, said to be French for "to sway back and forth," occurs when something like a sudden wind or atmospheric pressure change causes part of the lake's surface to be depressed. The water piles up elsewhere and then runs back to seek its level in a regular oscillation or sloshing that can go on for hours. The biggest seiche I've seen was about three feet. But some on Lake Ontario have been far bigger. Because of their shapes and orientations, Lakes Erie and Michigan can generate huge seiches—ten feet

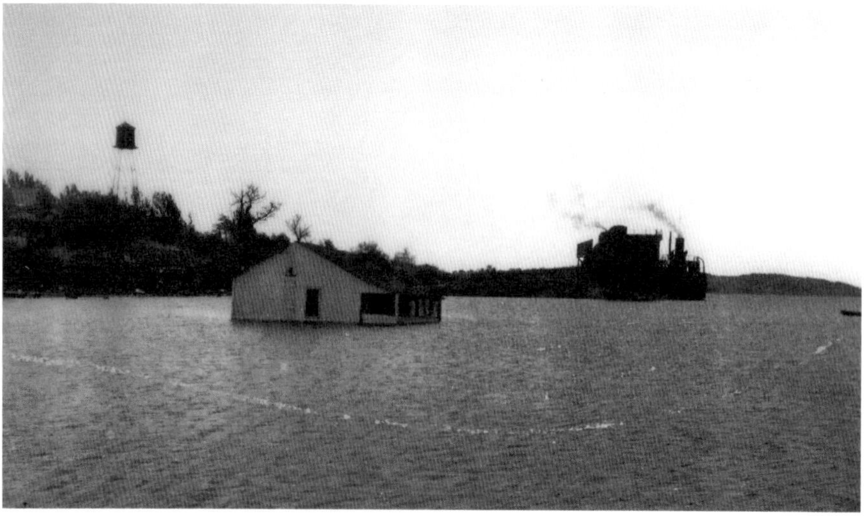

In the 1920s, this cottage was pushed off the barrier bar and into Fair Haven Bay by a seiche. *Sterling Historical Society.*

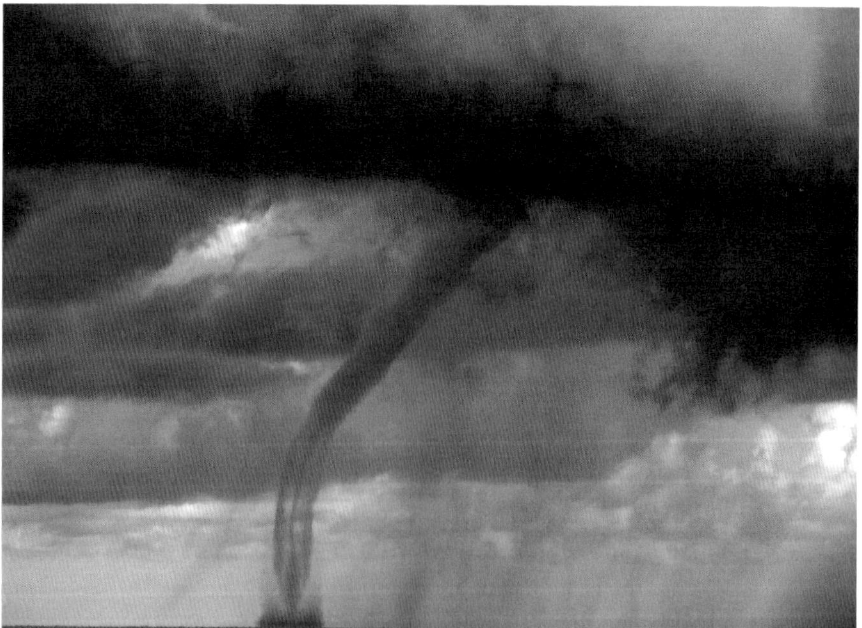

This late summer waterspout was photographed on Lake Ontario recently. *International Centre for Waterspout Research.*

or more having been recorded there. On May 27, 2012, the *Cleveland News* reported, "A 7-foot seiche wave crashed over the break wall and swept some children out into the lake over the break wall as the water returned back to the lake." (The kids were rescued.)

Weather events on the lake have prompted many tales. Perhaps twenty years ago, I was sailing down the St. Lawrence on a squally, unsettled afternoon when a dark cloud swept overhead and dumped a brief deluge of rain on my boat. After it stopped, I was bemused by the presence of many small, gelatinous blobs on the boat's cabin top mixed with bits of pondweed. Close examination revealed them to be snail egg masses. Later that day, I talked to another boat skipper who had experienced a similar fallout of plant and animal life. We decided that the blustery weather had probably produced a short-lived waterspout somewhere nearby. The small sea-going tornado must have crossed a backwater and carried some of it aloft. When the waterspout broke up, it dropped the water and associated biota as rain. The odd occurrences of frogs and fish falling from the sky that are reported now and then from around the country must surely be of similar causes.

Waterspouts, ephemeral and mysterious as they may be, are actually fairly common on Lake Ontario. A couple years ago, a September cold front generated 154 reports of waterspouts on all the Great Lakes, and in 2003, more than twenty were sighted in one week on Lake Ontario. They are most frequent in the fall when cold air rushes across the still warm lake. The sharp contrasts in temperature and associated strong turbulent energies can cause tornado-like funnels with up to seventy-mile-per-hour winds—strong enough to damage an unprepared sailing vessel. The dark tendrils drop from clouds and often stretch and bend, almost like living creatures. Waterspouts have been blamed for some sea monster sightings, and they are so odd and so short-lived that they might well appear to be a bizarre life form if seen at close range by an exhausted mariner during bad weather and poor visibility. Now that so many beachcombers and boat operators have smart phone cameras, research on their formation and occurrence is getting a boost from citizen science documentation. The International Centre for Waterspout Research has a website that collects and logs reports from the general public as part of its effort.

But some mysterious phenomena on the lake defy explanation. At least one cargo schooner is said to have been found suddenly abandoned with sails still set and no one aboard. And numerous unexplained losses of ships and planes exist in the history of Lake Ontario. The sudden loss of the schooner *Emerald* with all hands back in 1903 on a not so windy night still puzzles historians. There has even been a book devoted to the paranormal mysteries of Lake Ontario: *Gateway to Oblivion: The Great Lakes Bermuda Triangle*, by Hugh Cochrane. Cochrane writes of the lake's east end as being "a place of eerie negative emissions," according to psychic observers. He also describes numerous UFO sightings. Many of the Lake Ontario ship losses discussed in his book can be explained by unfortunate geography, weather or human error, but some of the UFOs he details defy analysis. And they continue to be seen. A book came out a few years ago titled *Underground Alien Bases*, by "Commander X," that describes a possible subterranean UFO base in the Toronto area.

Gateway to Oblivion contains descriptions of dozens of perplexing sightings seen over the lake. Many appear as airborne lights, often changing color and flashing on and off. In the summer of 1974 and again in 1975, there was a veritable plague of UFOs at the lake's west end. Observers reported disk- or cigar shaped-shaped objects. One person saw a UFO with a domed top that glowed orange. Other witnesses saw bright lights out over the lake. To some viewers, the lights moved with little apparent purpose, while others saw lights that "gave the impression they were under intelligent control."

Cochrane says, in the spring of 1975, the *Hamilton Spectator* printed a photo of a disk-shaped UFO, and his book also contains a time exposure taken of some of the lights then seen over the water near Niagara on the Lake. The photographer set up his tripod and opened his shutter for a long exposure. The result was a shot looking across the water toward Toronto, showing the city skyline with five streaks of light, some of which showed abrupt course changes, in the sky above. Cochrane states that a call to the Toronto airport showed no commercial aircrafts were then present in the area, and the brightness and abrupt turns and halts seen in the photo suggested something other than a commercial aircraft was flying through the night sky that spring.

More reports of sightings appeared in the local papers in 1976 and 1977. A UFO was seen hovering over the Lennox generating station at the upper Gap on the Bay of Quinte, and just north of Lake Ontario, several scorched rings about thirty feet across were found in grassy fields. On January 8, 1977, a Napanee newspaper reported that someone had sighted a forty-foot, disk-shaped object hovering at treetop height and making a droning sound. Three bright yellow lights glowed around its rim, and it appeared to be rotating counterclockwise.

Other than just plain honest error, delusion or fireballs from space junk and meteors, I can offer no very convincing explanations as to what these UFOs could possibly be. I have seen a bright star low on the horizon go through vivid color changes, turning from red to blue to green in a few seconds. And I have focused on a star and thought it was moving when in fact I was moving, making it seem to shift position. Some UFO sightings might be of stars or meteors or satellites misinterpreted by observers in the darkness. A couple years ago, I was standing watch aboard a topsail schooner sailing the Gulf of Maine when a fellow crew member called out the sighting of the red port side running light of a converging vessel. To our mutual amusement, it turned out to be the light of a ruddy rising moon, low on the horizon, peeking through a small break in the cloud. Once off busy New York Harbor, I saw the approaching bright white masthead light of a ship heading straight for me in the predawn darkness. It took me five minutes to realize I was actually seeing Venus rising over the black ocean horizon.

Globes of light over rivers or marshes might be swamp gas, and Marcel Minnaert, in *Light and Color in the Outdoors*, writes of a UFO that turned out to be an owl. While in its nest hole, the bird had gotten bits of rotten wood on its feathers, wood that was host to a bio luminescent fungus. The resulting eerie greenish glow was visible in the night sky as the bird flew overhead. It might seem farfetched to mistake an owl for a UFO, but it is extremely difficult to judge the distance or size of an object in the sky with no other reference points nearby. I've seen glowing "fox fire" fungus on a rotting log that was amazingly bright to eyes adapted to darkness. So a glowing owl could make a credible UFO.

But some UFOs are so spectacular and so peculiar that nothing other than an imagination run wild seems to explain them. Cochrane offers a couple of tries, though. One, also touted by "Commander X" in his book, is that there really are extraterrestrial pilots using underwater areas as bases of operation. Perhaps they are even establishing a submarine staging area off Niagara Falls at the lake's west end.

Cochrane's other "theory" to explain the burned rings and ionizing glows seen in night skies over the lake is that "unexplained electromagnetic forces" periodically well up from the lake's bottom to form columns of raw energy that rise high into the air. Or, he theorizes, an invisible vortex of force erupts intermittently. He calls this phenomenon the Marysburg Vortex but is a little vague on the actual physics involved; however, he offers as one bit of evidence the existence of numerous magnetic anomalies present in the area (which are indeed noted on current nautical charts) along with the UFO sightings and the mysterious losses of dozens of aircraft and several ships. One such mysterious loss cited by Cochrane was the sudden disappearance of the schooner *Speedy*, described in chapter three.

In his quest to learn more about these anomalies, Cochrane contacted a noted dowser whose past credits included finding two hikers lost in the White Mountains. Given a map of Lake Ontario, the seer produced a series of drawings of what he believed were "flows of energy" that crossed the lake. Some of these terminated in energy "eruptions." Interestingly, one of these "energy flows" corresponds closely to a known fault under the lake's west end that has been studied because of concern about its possible impact on the Pickering nuclear reactors.

Cochrane asked a Canadian psychic living about eighty miles from Lake Ontario if she sensed anything unusual about the region. She answered that there seemed to be a negative force at its southeast end, adding it was as if this area were touched with a very strong radiation that still lingered so that nothing flourished there as it should. Maybe Cochrane's psychic was picking up a "vortex" in Mexico Bay, one of Lake Ontario's best-known graveyards for shipwrecks thanks to its location at the lake's lee end. Perhaps she knew of a little radioactive indiscretion at the Nine Mile One nuke that the rest of us missed. There were reports of an unusual number of aborted calves back in the 1970s in Scriba not long after the plant went on line and the staff was still in its operational learning curve. Who knows? I know I will take a lucky rock with me next summer when I sail through the Marysburg Vortex on the way to Kingston!

Perhaps less mysterious than a UFO but still wondrous to see is one of the lake's more dramatic mirages. They occur most often in April, May and June, when the chill of winter lingers within Lake Ontario's dark depths and long hours of strengthening sun warm the air. Mirages are most likely whenever there is a sharp contrast in temperatures between air and water. Often they show land normally invisible below the horizon as a dim narrow blue band just over the water. It may look like a fog bank or a dark streak. Sometimes, too, you may see a magnified or distorted boat in the distance. Mirages on the lake can be spectacular. An old neighbor of mine told of seeing a mirage of the Canadian shore on a bitter cold winter morning many years ago. The landscape was greatly magnified and so sharply detailed that she could even see cars moving along the streets. And the whole landscape appeared to be upside down. Another dramatic winter mirage of Canada made the Rochester newspaper in the 1880s.

In 1856, the *Lockport Journal* reported an August mirage. The description is quoted in *Great Lakes Shipwrecks* by William Ratigan: "It occurred just as the sun was setting, at which time some twelve vessels were seen reflected on the horizon, in an inverted position, with a distinctness and vividness truly

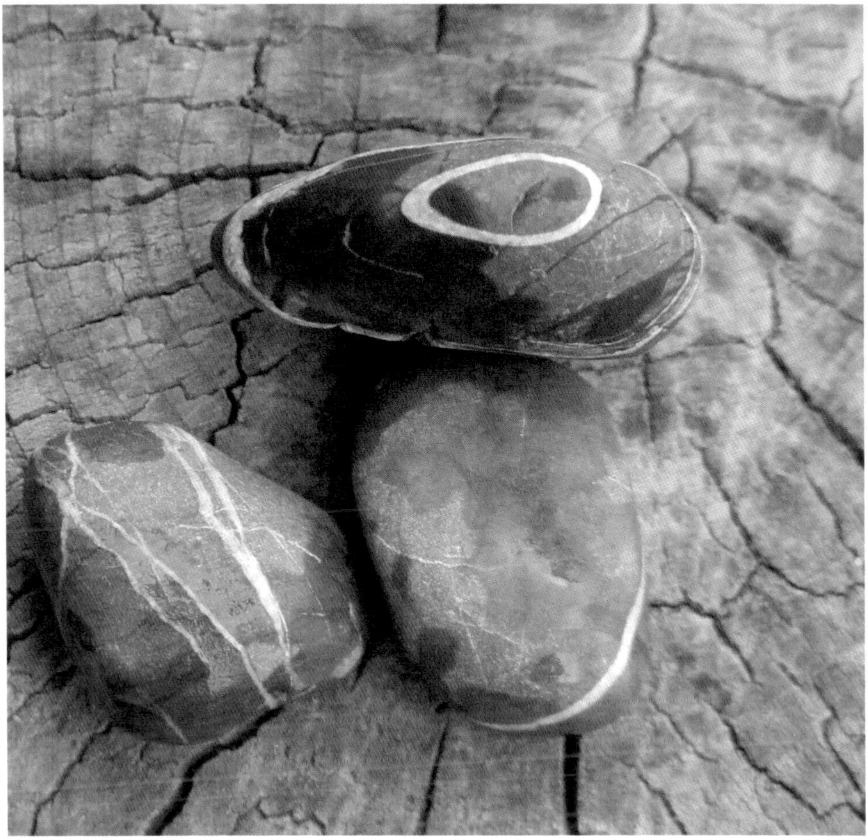

A Lake Ontario lucky rock is a black pebble with a white ring around it. *Author's collection.*

surprising. The atmosphere was overcast with a thick haze such as precedes a storm, and of a color favorable to represent upon the darkened background, vividly, the full outlines of the rigging, sails, etc., as perfect as if the ships themselves were actually transformed to the aerial canvas."

Last spring, I saw several striking mirages while out sailing. The first occurred on a bright sunny afternoon of light wind and cold water. Upon coming about and heading toward homeport, the shore before us suddenly transformed. Distant flat topped mesas and huge buttes of tawny brown and dark green now towered many hundreds of feet in the air. A few isolated spires and columns also appeared, and the more distant headlands showed a distinct horizontal dark line like a layer of smoke trailing off over the water from the top of the mountainous horizon. Occasionally, as I studied this

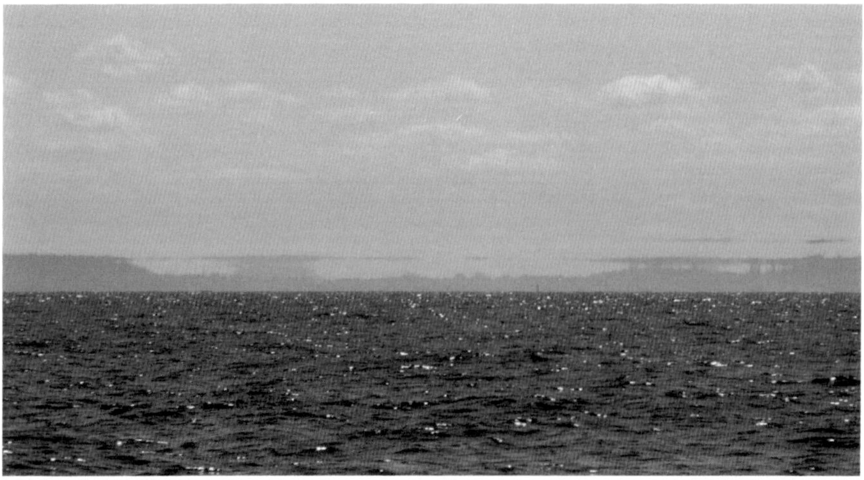

Looming mirage on Lake Ontario. *Author's collection.*

improbable stretch of shore, a little piece of a mesa top would detach itself and seem to float up and dwindle away. The whole thing kept changing continually, but the shifts were so gradual and subtle that it was almost impossible to track them. It was as if the front range of the Rockies blended with Monument Valley had suddenly erupted out of the lake.

A few days later, another mirage appeared on a sunny May afternoon of light wind and cold water. I looked off to the northeast and spotted Oswego's regular weekly cement boat leaving port. Only today, he had a consort, a second gray-hulled cement boat suspended directly above him and upside down. Both boats also appeared somewhat magnified, but neither was distorted, as the shoreline we'd seen a few days before had been. Quite the contrary, the boats appeared very sharply detailed and distinct on this bright but chilly afternoon.

There are, of course, well-understood explanations for these phenomena. Marcel Minnaert's marvelous book *Light and Color in the Outdoors* has excellent explanations of various mirages, as does the website Atmospheric Optics. Lake Ontario mirages are usually the "superior" type, in which something below the horizon appears to float above it inverted. The "inferior" mirage occurs when cold air lies over a sharply warmer surface, such as a concrete road or a large area of desert basin. A temperature difference of ten to twenty degrees Fahrenheit is necessary to see a really strong mirage. The silvery puddle on the road effect is actually the distant sky being reflected by these sharply different air layers acting as a lenses to bend the light. The best conditions for seeing a mirage on the lake are calm days when there isn't a lot of wind to stir up and mix the atmosphere near the lake surface.

Minnaert's book contains a photo of a mirage very much like those I've seen over the lake. It shows an island with several inverted and compressed images hanging above it. If more than one layer of air of different temperature lies over the water, you may get these multiple images, and they are also sensitive to the height of the observer. You can change the mirage appearance by climbing or descending just a few yards.

Mirages have been invoked to explain vanishing islands, but on Lake Ontario there may be other explanations for disappearing landforms. The lake appears to have had at least three vanishing islands plus one disappearing rock, the Devil's Horseblock (see chapter three). Samuel de Champlain did some early mapping of the area while visiting here, and one of his maps shows two large islands within Lake Ontario. One was located near the American shore by the mouth of the Niagara River; the other was on the Canadian side, not far from Cobourg in the neighborhood of the Devil's Horseblock. This island appeared to be about fifteen miles long and several miles wide. Older charts of Fair Haven Bay sometimes show an actual island where the "Grassy Island" shoal is located today. Another instance of a vanished island on the lake occurs in the historical novel *Northwest Passage* by Kenneth Roberts, in which the characters meet on an island three miles west of Oswego about where Ford Shoal is today.

Changes in water level combined with erosion might account for these vanished lands. The lake levels fluctuated a great deal more in the early days of settlement when no power dam existed on the St. Lawrence to control lake flows. Extreme levels might well have created islands or eliminated them rapidly. Even today, the bluffs along the south and southeast sections of the lake coast erode at a rate of three to five feet a year, so a powerful storm during extreme high water could wash away a low-lying island in a few hours.

Mysterious mirages and UFOs are still occasionally part of Lake Ontario landscape. But it's been many years since a sea monster has put in an appearance here. Sea monsters were the UFOs of the nineteenth century. Strange beasts were then sighted frequently in both salt and fresh water, and they came in as many varieties as today's UFO. One saltwater sighting reported by an angler in the late nineteenth century was of an eighty-foot-long beast that spouted blue flames from two hornlike structures near the center of its head. Other witnesses reported huge serpents that swam at astonishing speeds or what appeared to be gigantic octopi or squids.

Monstrous creatures and secretive beasts have a powerful pull on the psyche. We have a need for a little mystery in our lives. Mysterious rites are well entrenched in religious and fraternal orders and in many other aspects of society. I admit that there are times when looking at the apparently limitless expanses of the lake that I wish we did have an unknown beast or two prowling its deeper, darker realms. I'm not the only one, either. A few months ago, I was visiting with a neighbor, a retired commercial diver who shared a story: "Whenever we would dive on a dam, after we came up, the locals would ask, 'You guys see any fish down there?' We'd always tell them, 'Oh yeah! There's huge fish down there. There's catfish six feet long with mouths a foot wide. Catfish that could swallow a basket ball!'

"Then maybe a year or two later we'd be back there again, maybe in a bar having a beer after work, and someone would hear we're working out on this particular dam, and they would say, 'I hear there's some huge catfish out there.' So whenever you hear a giant catfish story, you know some diver started that," he told me with a twinkle in his eye.

Last fall the same neighbor also told me quite seriously that his son and grandson had seen an odd creature by the west jetty of the Fair Haven channel. It appeared to be perhaps fifteen feet long as it swam near the surface. It had two fins, one near the head and one located far aft, and it just "hung around the entrance to the bay," he said. What could it have been, he wondered. Perhaps two big salmon swimming together had made this "monster." Or perhaps it was something else altogether different and unknown.

In the late nineteenth century, there were so many giant fish and sea serpent stories from salt water on the East Coast that a veritable monster fever swept the country. Lake Champlain's beast was seen a number of times in the late 1800s, and at least a half dozen other lakes in North America have been said to contain large and possibly dangerous beasts of unknown species. A very respectable body of literature (and some photos) have accumulated around "Champ," Champlain's resident monster.

The prime habitat of freshwater monsters seems to be large, deep and cold lakes. Flat Head Lake, Lake Okanagan. In Scotland, ancient stone carvings from the time of the Picts near Lock Ness show a variety of well-rendered, realistic animals. All are readily recognizable except for one—a peculiar creature with a large body, limblike flippers and a long neck. Africa, Scandinavia and even Australia have lakes with stories of strange beasties within their depths. Some reports of monster sightings have been sparked by local hotel and resort operators hoping to build trade. A fairly elaborate hoax, complete with a homemade monster crafted by a hotel owner who wanted to

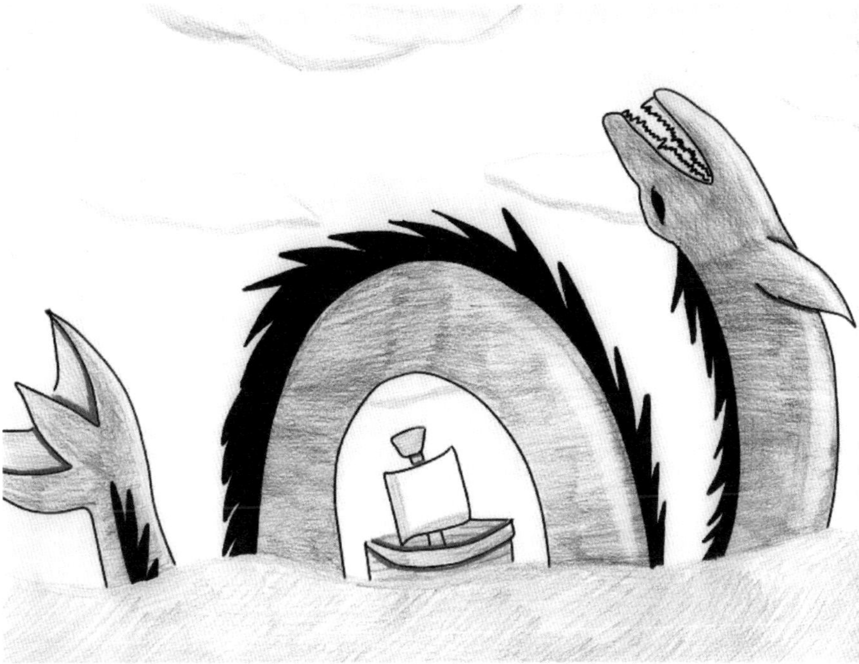

Lake Monster. *By Katie Dawson.*

boost business, took place on Silver Lake around 1850. The scheme worked for one summer, with thousands coming to see the alleged twenty-foot-long greenish serpent. Years later, a canvas and wire contraption—the remains of the "serpent"—were discovered in the attic of the lakeshore Walker House Hotel. And to this day, Champ is touted as an attraction for Lake Champlain visitors by the local chamber of commerce.

Richard Palmer, a historian of Lake Ontario maritime affairs, contributed the following monster tale published in the *Oswego Palladium* on July 1, 1833. It may not be coincidence that these snakelike monsters resemble the horned serpents of Iroquois stories:

> *Our office has been favored with a visit from Captain Abijah Kellogg of the schooner* Polythermus, *of Sacket's, arrived this morning from Rochester. This gentleman has related to us such a tale of wonder, a tale so incredible, that we scruple some, as the Yankees say it, laying his narration before our readers, lest they might think it but the creation of your imagination. Capt. Kellogg states:*

Yesterday evening (June 15th) about 7 o'clock, as he was making for Kingston harbor, the "Ducks" bearing N. by W. distant two miles, he saw something lying still on the weather bow that looked like the mast of a vessel. Observing it more attentively, he was surprised and alarmed to see it in motion, and steering towards the schooner.

Singing out to his hands to take care of themselves, he put the schooner up to the wind, lashed the helm a lee, and run up the main rigging, waiting for the monster to approach. The serpent, for it was no other than an immense snake, neared the vessel fast and passed immediately under her stern, taking no notice whatever of the schooner or those on board, but affording to every body an ample opportunity to observe and note his monstrous dimensions.

In length he was about 175 feet, of a dark blue color, spotted with brown; towards either end he tapered off, but about the middle his body was of the circumference of a flour barrel, his head was peculiarly small and could not well be distinguished but from the direction in which he moved. He swam with an undulating movement, keeping the best part of his body underwater, but occasionally showing his entire length. He was in sight full fifteen minutes and when last seen was making the best of his way down the St. Lawrence. On board the schooner were two young men, the vessel's crew, together with three passengers, who are willing to be qualified to the truth of what has been here stated.

Richard Palmer also contributed this 1877 *Oswego Palladium* account of a serpent that had overindulged the night before on corn mash at a Canadian whiskey distillery:

In the summer of '40, I think it was, a schooner I was in cut a sea sarpint [sic] *in two. We stood out from Kingston about noon with the wind from the nor'east, a pipin' rather strong, and as the schooner was flyin' light, she traveled astonishin' to see. Just after passin' the Ducks the 'old man,' who was pacin' the deck, called the mate's attention to sumptin' in the water about a quarter of a mile dead ahead. Lookin' off that way a long object, resemblin' the back of a shoal, was plainly seen. For a minute or two the 'old man' was in doubt what to do, but finally concludin' that a shoal had no business in such a place, he ordered the man at the wheel to steer dead for it.*

All of us on deck, exceptin' the man at the wheel, run for'ard to get a sight of the obstruction and got on the forecastle deck jest in time to see that the thing was nothin' more nor less than a huge sea sarpint, sound asleep.

The monster wasn't less'n fifty feet long, with a head sumthin' similar to that of the fiery dragon we see in picter [sic] *books. It was a full dull brown color, scales on its back, hair jest back of the neck, and a tail like a harpoon head. In less time than it takes to tell it, we was atop the monster and crushin' its bones in an awful way.*

Our headway was deadened a trifle but we kept on, and as the monster came up under our stern, we could see we had cut it clean in two and the two halves was swimmin' away in opposite directions. Before then, there hadn't been but one sea sarpint on Lake Ontario, but since then two have been seen most every year. Morton's distillery, near Kingston, was in full blast at that time, and I account for the sarpint bein' asleep this side of the Ducks instead of the other side of Snake Island, its usual haunt, by the fact that that mornin' the men at the distillery dumped two or three hundred bushels of mash into the lake and the sarpint had got a trifle 'how come you so.'

A more recent monster sighting dates from 1902. On that occasion, George Adams of Fair Haven, an elderly but still sharp-sighted gentleman, went down to the shore of the bay to do some pickerel fishing on a September morning. To his amazement, he saw a creature swimming out in the bay. It was perhaps fifteen to twenty feet long and showed a bit of spray and spouting around its head. He hurried into town to tell one and all of his sighting, his credibility being enhanced by the fact that he was a veteran of the Union army who served with Sheridan as an eagle-eyed scout.

Several people gathered on the shore hoping for a glimpse of the beast, but it had vanished. Alas, for the world of mystery, later that day, the editor of the local paper heard of the sighting and did a little investigative footwork. He learned that a red and white milk cow, pastured on Hunt's Point, had been attacked by bees. She stampeded into the bay and swam across East Cove, apparently being sighted en route by Mr. Adams.

In all fairness to Adams, I once saw a deer swimming on a course parallel to my boat about a hundred feet away and couldn't for the life of me figure out what it was until I got within a few yards of it, so odd and unexpected a sight it was. And some of the snakelike-creature sightings might also have a basis in fact. On a glassy, calm day, an isolated wave generated by a distant ship can travel many miles, and its dark ripple across the surface looks very much like a rapidly swimming giant snake. In the nineteenth century, the lake really did have a "monster" fish of sorts: the sturgeon. These sluggish brown fish grew up to nine feet long and sometimes foraged in the lake's then

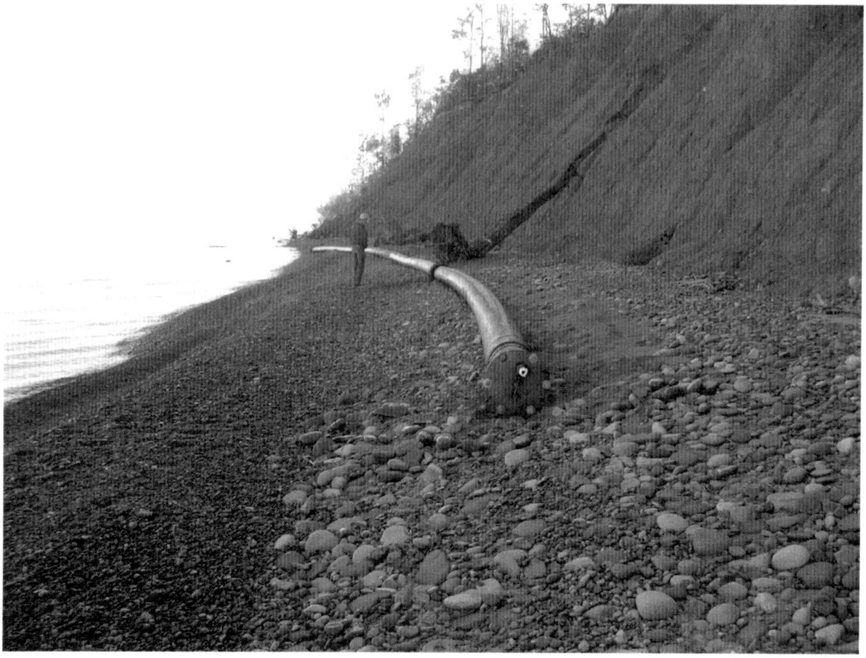

Stranded sea serpent. Presumably it expired after spawning; note bumps on the head characteristic of this species, *Polyvinyl tuberosis*. *Author's collection.*

clear shallows, where they'd be readily seen. Monster sightings on the Great Lakes have generally turned out to actually be sightings of carp, salmon swimming at the surface in formation near each other or pure mirages. But maybe there really is something down there.

At the end the last ice age, there was a period when the level of Lake Ontario's basin was well below that of present day. At that time, salt water reached far up the river so that the St. Lawrence was an arm of the sea and Lakes Champlain and Ontario were accessible to saltwater creatures. That so-called marine invasion left our lake with several species of fish that adapted to freshwater life and continued to thrive. The original Atlantic salmon population, the deep-water sculpin and the little shrimp *Mysis* were all originally marine species that adapted to life in the lake. Perhaps a few plesiosaurs or a basilosaurus or two were also trapped after the land rebounded from the weight of the glaciers and the lakes again became fresh.

Many of the twentieth-century sightings of Nessie, Champ and other lake monsters describe the creatures as being about thirty feet long with a humped body, a long neck and a small head. Other sightings describe a large serpent- or eel-like creature, sometimes with a large horselike head. The first description roughly fits the best guess as to what the fish-eating plesiosaurs looked like. The second could conceivably match up with an elongated snakelike primitive whale, such as the basilosaurus, an air breather that lived as recently as thirty million years ago in salt water. I admit that, with all the sonar studies that are run annually on Lake Ontario for biological surveys, it seems pretty unlikely that we could overlook anything as big as either of these beasts. But maybe they are just really good at avoiding the boats that conduct the surveys. Perhaps the lack of recent sightings here is explained simply by the lake's shear size. And except for a month or two in the summer, its waters ten or twenty miles off shore host relatively little boat traffic.

One wonders, with so many monster stories, some dating back to the days of the Iroquois who feared giant grub- or sluglike creatures said to live at the bottom of some of our lakes, whether some of these tales have been founded on actual sightings. We of western tradition, with our written records, have often dismissed Indian legends based on oral history as being unreliable. Yet some of their stories appear to preserve detailed, accurate and historically verifiable information for very long periods. When Samuel de Champlain met with tribes on the St. Lawrence in the 1600s, he found stories of Cartier's visit from nearly a century before. The tribes gave accounts of trading for steel tools and of eating hard tack and drinking red wine then. (The storytellers recounted the red wine as being blood and the hard tack as being wood).

The Jesuit chronicler Pierre Charlevoix recorded in the 1700s an Indian tale of a giant "elk" with long reddish hair and legs so long it could walk easily through deep snow. This "elk," he was told, had an arm somewhat like that of a man. Charlevoix's account reads, in part, that "there is also a very diverting tradition among the Indians of a great elk, of such a monstrous size that the rest are like pismires in comparison of him; his legs, say they, are so long that eight feet of snow are not the least incumbrance [*sic*] to him. His hide is proof against all manner of weapons, and he has a sort of arm proceeding from his shoulders which he uses as we do ours. He is always attended by a vast number of elks which form his court and which render him all the services he requires." Allowing for the vagaries of translation and time, this sounds to me like a pretty fair description of an ice age mastodon or mammoth, both of which were present in the Lake Ontario region when the first paleo-Indians also lived here. So perhaps in the past, there were strange beasts living in the lake's depths that were also remembered in Native American legend and story.

Large animals can remain hidden from science for many years only to be discovered by pure chance. The lobe-finned coelacanth, a deep-sea fish that grows to six feet, was "discovered" quite recently. And the deep-sea giant squid was first photographed alive just a few years ago. An antelopelike animal new to science showed up in Asia recently, and several bizarre previously unknown anaerobic bacteria were found in caves, including mass colonies of something the explorers called snot-ites that dripped sulfuric acid on them. So who really knows what might lurk in the lake's depths? Mysteries and wonders do still remain on this amazing world of ours.

CHAPTER 3

SHORELINE LORE

The Power of a Name

Humans like to name things—cats, dogs, boats, homesteads, hurricanes and prominent geographic features have all been distinguished with names. Landmark names give a sense of place. Once, when we lived close to the land, our very identities and ways of thinking were intimately tied to the places we lived in. Names were part of that cultural landscape.

Many of our upstate New York names are "recycled" ones that arrived with the European settlers. Others, though, given by the people who lived here before us, are unique to our area. Most of the 1,800-odd islands of the Thousand Islands region have names, as do dozens of other islands, shoals, points, bays and landmarks on and around the lake. Each name has some sort of story associated with it.

Some of those stories are simple and short. It's not hard to imagine, for example, how Presqu'ile Bay's Calf Pasture Point (now grown up with scrub red cedar) got its name. Other name origins are more obscure, like that of Twelve O'Clock Point at the west end of the Bay of Quinte, a few miles from Calf Pasture Point. Originally, before the Murray Canal was built, the narrow stretch of land between the Bay of Quinte and Presqu'ile Bay was a portage. Later, a primitive wooden railway was constructed to haul small cargo boats overland, and the crews usually reached the east end of the portage by noon, hence the name.

Some place names, like Charity Shoal or the Devil's Nose, have well-documented and unfortunate origins. Shoals and dangerous rocks on the lake were often named for the first vessel unlucky enough to find them. But

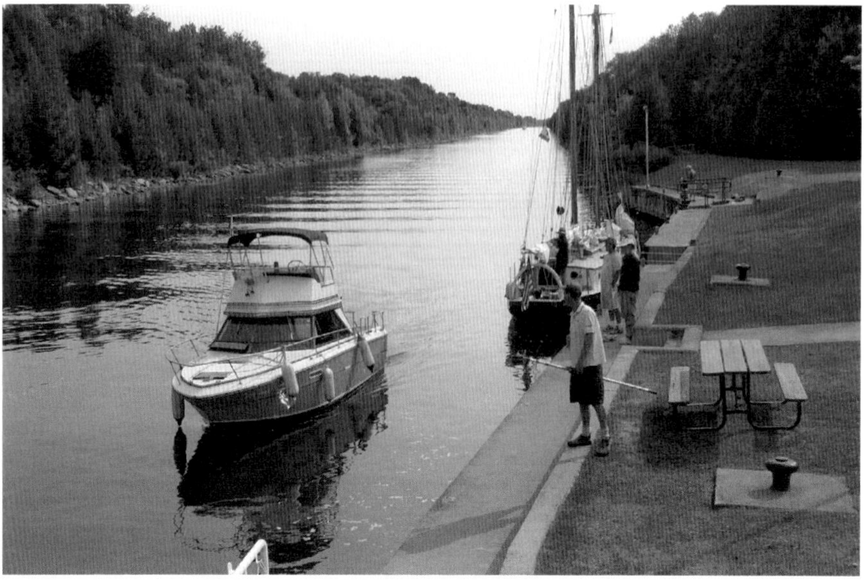

Murray Canal near Twelve O'Clock Point. The man with the pole is the bridge tender. The pole has a small box on the end that he extends to collect tolls. *Author's collection.*

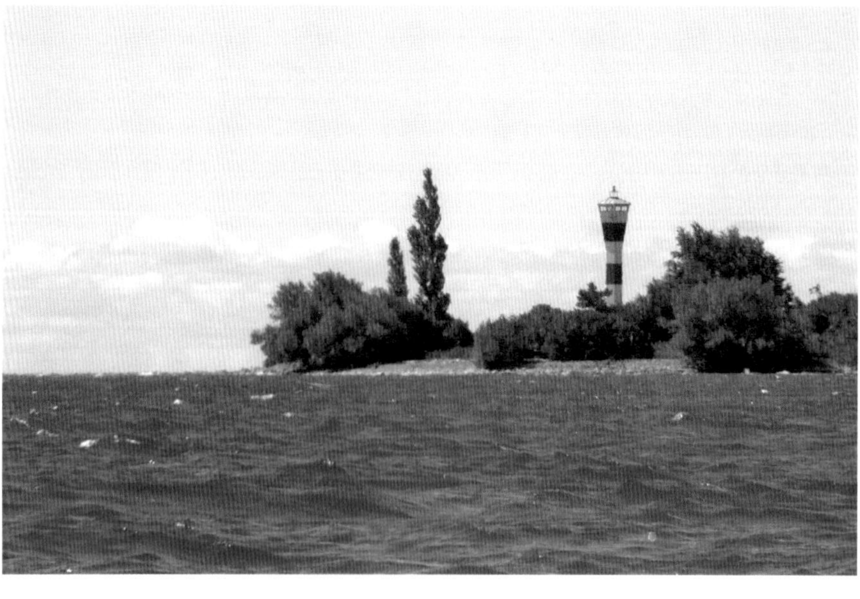

Swetman Island light on its east end warns ships of the extensive shoals between the island and Long Point. One of the first lighthouses on the lake was built here in 1829. *Author's collection.*

the stories behind other landmark names may never be known. One wonders for whom Sheba's Island in West Lake is named. "Sheba" hardly sounds like a good old Loyalist family name. How the cove just east of Wicked Point of Prince Edward County came to be called Soup Harbor is still up for speculation as well. Perhaps a barley-laden schooner hit the rocks of aptly named Wicked Point in some long-ago storm and went to pieces, causing her grain cargo to collect in the neighboring cove to create a cold-water gruel.

Many landmarks and important features have simple descriptive names, Stony and Grape Islands or Gull Bar being examples. (Today, Gull Bar next to Swetman Island usually has at least as many cormorants as gulls on it.) A couple of the larger, more important islands are named after important people, such as Wolfe (named for the British general James Wolfe, whose victory at Quebec helped shorten the French and Indian War) and Amherst (named after another British military leader, Jeffrey Amherst, who captured Montreal to end the war). Other islands, such as Swetman and Ward's, are named for past owners and human associates. Swetman Island is also called False Duck Island, as it was sometimes confused with nearby Main Duck.

A few lake landmarks have retained names given to them by people who lived here before the British. Waupoos Island, which is just off Prince Edward County, is named for the native word for "rabbit," and the Oswego River gets its name from a native word loosely translated as: "Where the water flows out." Irondequoit Bay is supposed to have been "where the water turns aside" in the Seneca language, and Sodus Bay may have been a corruption of *Asserodus*, "silvery water" to the Cayugas.

Though many names' origins remain uncertain, those of some landmarks along the shore and in the lake itself are well documented. The Devil's Nose, for example, is a prominent high point that rises above the low, flat lake plain around it on the lake's south shore near Hamlin Beach State Park. It lies about thirteen miles west of Braddock's Bay near Rochester, and a rocky shoal extends a good half mile off shore from it. These submerged rocks, the remains of eroded land that once thrust much farther north into the lake, have caused several Lake Ontario shipwrecks. This particular stretch of shoreline is generally pretty free of offshore hazards, and in the early days of commerce especially, eighteenth-century mariners sailing on uncharted waters often coasted close along the shore, making them vulnerable to odd outlying shoals like this one. The *Duchess of York* hit this rocky area with a number of troops aboard in November 1799 and soon went to pieces. Captain Van Cleve did a sketch of the wreck that shows red-coated soldiers struggling ashore from the ship.

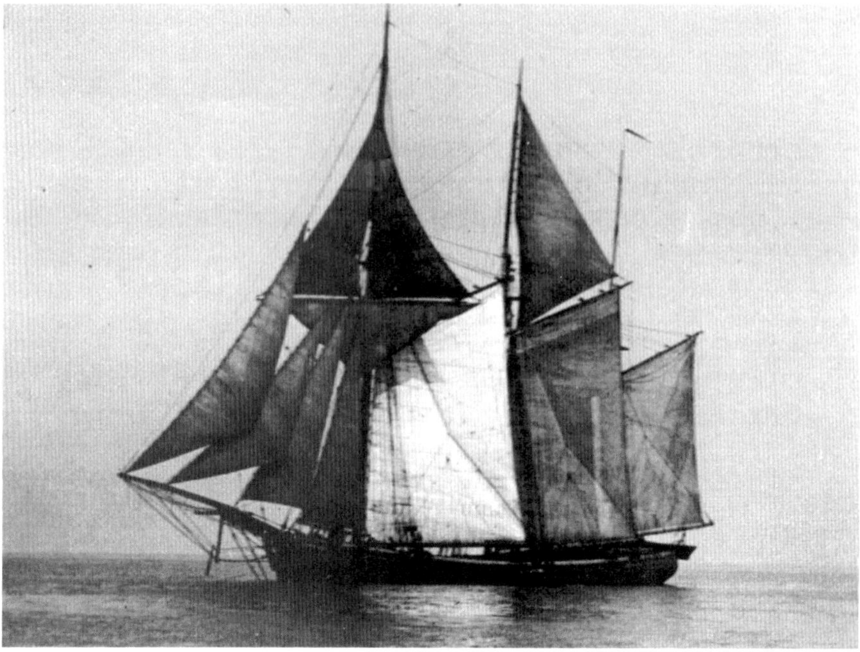

The *Reuban Doud* a few years before her end, seen here under sail off Toronto. *Photo supplied by Walter Lewis.*

Even after the lake was well charted, the shoal continued to take its toll. The *Reuben Doud*, one of the few survivors of the age of sail that made it into the twentieth century, went ashore there in 1903. After shoveling most of the coal cargo overboard, her crew got her off with the help of a couple tugs. Just two years later, she went on the beach at Ward's Island off Toronto and broke up.

The Devil's Horseblock is a Lake Ontario landmark that has vanished. It was a large rock outcrop that lay a few inches below the water surface and stood several miles off shore and a little west of Presqu'ile Bay. Its discoverer described it as being a column or massive pillar of limestone that rose fifty feet from the lake's bottom. It was responsible for the famous wreck of the schooner *Speedy* that took place in 1803.

Ed Burtt, a diver and underwater explorer who discovered the *Speedy*'s remains a few years ago, explained in a phone interview that the rock's name came from the round outline of the outcrop as seen on a chart. It closely resembled the weights once used to tether animals for short periods, and Burtt suggested an adjacent shoal looked a bit like a horse's head when viewed on the map.

The wreck of the HMS *Speedy* is a story with a dash of the supernatural. Several written versions of her loss exist, and this is adapted from accounts by C.H.J. Snider and Robert Townsend. The story begins when a murder occurred in the sparsely settled frontier lands of southern Ontario. The victim was a white man, a fur trapper and trader, and the act took place at an isolated trading post on the shores of Lake Scugog, about twenty miles north from Lake Ontario. The victim, John Sharpe, formerly a soldier in the Queen's Rangers regiment, apparently was the innocent and unlucky victim of a revenge killing.

Ogetonicut, an Objibwa Indian, bashed Sharpe's brains out to avenge the death of his brother, Whistling Duck. Ogetonicut's brother had been killed at the hands of a white man some twelve months before. Fearing retribution from the increasingly powerful Europeans, the band's chief reluctantly turned Ogetonicut over to the governor at old Fort York, where Toronto stands on Lake Ontario's shore today.

Ogetonicut had admitted to the crime, and the evidence of a brutal death by bludgeoning was clear and undeniable. But the Indian couldn't be tried, convicted and hanged in York. He had to be convicted in the district where the murder had occurred. So the court and prisoner moved down the lake to the newly formed District of Newcastle near Presqu'ile Bay. Only then could Ogetonicut die at the end of the hangman's rope.

By the time the lawyers had all this worked out, it was early October, a time of changeable weather on the big lake. The only practical means of transporting the prisoner, lawyers, Indian interpreters, bailiff, judge and other assorted legal personages involved was by means of the government schooner *Speedy*.

Speedy was a small two-master, sixty feet on deck, and had launched only eight years before, but already she was riddled with dry rot. Built of unseasoned oak and pine, her condition was common to many early Lake Ontario vessels. The crew manned the pumps even in fair weather, and just a few months before, her commander, Thomas Paxton, had made port with so much water in his bilges that his cargo of Indian trade goods had been damaged. On this day, some twenty-odd passengers crowded aboard, and the rest of the company involved with the trial took to the tenuous trails along the forested lakeshore to make their way to Newcastle located on Presqu'ile peninsula.

The *Speedy* set sail on a quiet Sunday, October 7, with a moderate offshore breeze and smooth water. Her prisoner was locked into the forecastle, and as the schooner sailed slowly along the shore, she was watched by an

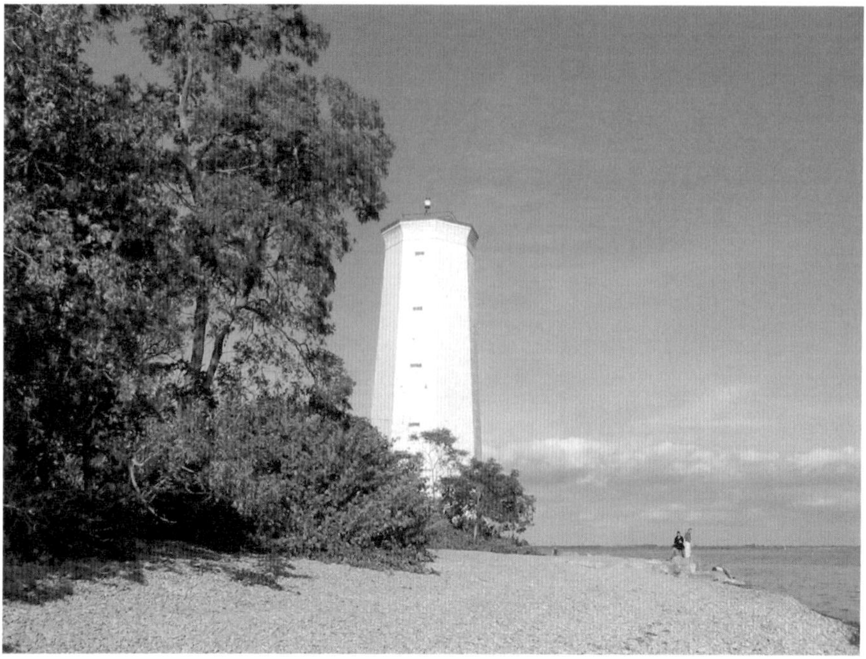

Presqu'ile Point Light marks the entrance to the harbor that the *Speedy* was trying to reach on that fateful night in 1803. *Photo supplied by Ed Burtt.*

old woman with burning black eyes. This was Bitterskin, the mother of both Ogetonicut, the murderer, and his hapless brother, Whistling Duck. Among her tribe, she had a reputation of being a witch of sorts, able to make medicine against those who were her enemies. This October day, she invoked the darkest powers of the wind makers and the giants inhabiting the lake's depths. She cried and beseeched them to stop the vessel that now carried her last son away to the gallows.

Days are short in early October, and when the light died, so did the wind. Morning found the *Speedy* becalmed off the marshes of what today is the city of Oshawa. Progress was scant that day, and when darkness fell, the *Speedy* was still four miles west of Presqu'ile Point. But the temperature and the glass (barometer) had dropped steadily all day, and shortly after nightfall, a few snowflakes drifted down out of the dark sky. Then a chill breath of wind wafted across the water and filled the *Speedy*'s sails, wind from almost dead ahead. Minutes later it was blowing a full gale from the northeast.

The *Speedy*'s five-man crew scrambled to reef and furl and then turned to man the pumps. But the water soon gained on their efforts. As Lieutenant

Paxton hardened up to tack the last four miles into port, he had two things very much on his mind: the rising water level in his bilges and the presence of, between him and safe harbor, an unmarked rock four miles offshore. Deadly and invisible, the stone snag lay just beneath the lake's surface. Had it been daylight, Paxton could have taken a bearing on three tall trees on the shore, lining them up with the end of Milligan's Beach to avoid the Devil's Horseblock. But in the windswept night, he could only head out into the lake close hauled and hope he was still west of the rock. He ordered a gun fired, and the watchers on shore anticipating his arrival responded by lighting a bonfire to mark the port's entrance.

Even under the land's lee in smooth water, the straining *Speedy* was taking on water. Fast. Soon she was so waterlogged that she wouldn't come up into the wind to tack. Paxton had to wear around and, in so doing, lost ground against the relentless wind. The watchers on shore heard and saw no more of the vessel. She simply vanished.

Almost certainly, the *Speedy* struck the Devil's Horseblock, possibly in answer to Bitterskin's prayers. A few days later, wreckage was reported from the south shore of the lake at the Devil's Nose that was positively identified as being from the *Speedy*. In the spring of 1805, Captain Selleck of Newcastle searched on a calm day with clear water and perfect thirty-foot visibility for the Devil's Horseblock. Despite his carefully plotted ranges from the year before, he could not find it. In 1817, during a lake-wide hydrographic survey, surveyors searched, again in vain, for the stone column four miles off shore. Did the collision with the *Speedy* cause it to partly fracture and fall to the bottom as a pile of rubble? For many years, writers speculated about the loss of the *Speedy* and where she went down. Her sudden disappearance, some suggested, had a touch of the supernatural about it.

Then in 1989, diver Ed Burtt of Belleville discovered a shipwreck off Presqu'ile. He found two masts, a broken hull and "cannon balls of the size required by the four pound cannons typically carried on provincial marine ships." Burtt explained that a wreck with cannons must predate the end of the War of 1812 because of a treaty between the United States and Britain that agreed to a ban on armed vessels on the lakes. Surveys also found manacles, a ball and chain and indicated that the hull was about sixty feet long. One of the most telling finds to date is the ship's bell, lying on the bottom with only the English letter *s* clearly visible. The *Speedy's* grave had been found.

Other dangerous shoals include those off Wicked Point, Ford Shoals just west of Oswego and the ledges around Main Duck and Galloo Islands.

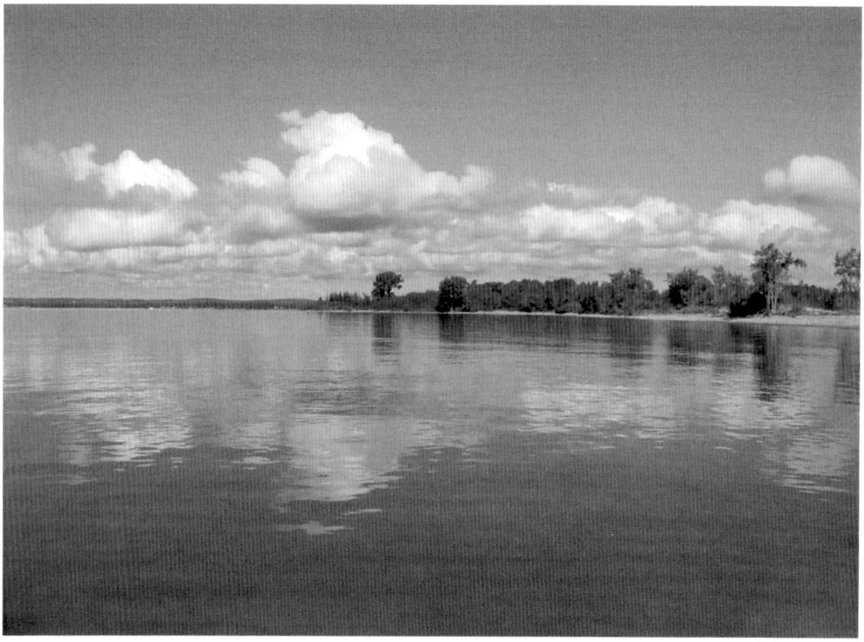

A local farmer salvaged planks and timbers from the shore near Presqu'ile Point, the remains of the *Speedy*, to use in a barn that still stands today. *Photo supplied by Ed Burtt.*

Charity, Moira, Ford and Psyche Shoals all bear the names of a schooner or steamer. Minnie Blakely Shoal was named for a small schooner scow from Port Credit that hit the rocks while carrying a cargo of ashes. (Hardwood ashes were a very marketable commodity when land was being cleared for farming. Ashes were steeped to produce lye that was then boiled down to create a residue of "black salts" that the early settlers then processed into potash for making soap or gun powder.)

Charity Shoal is a particularly odd rock pile. It lies right on the path that ships going in and out of the St. Lawrence would take and has claimed a number of victims. Like the Devil's Horseblock, there is also a hint of the paranormal about this geological formation. Some have claimed mysterious ship-killing forces surround its circular depression. A hydrological survey of the lake bottom made a few years ago describes it in dry scientific language as being "a small equidimensional circular depression 1000 meters in diameter, with a continuous encircling rim." Some of the rim lies within a few feet of the surface and looks strikingly like that of a meteor crater. Adding to its general mystery is the long-established "magnetic anomaly" marked on the

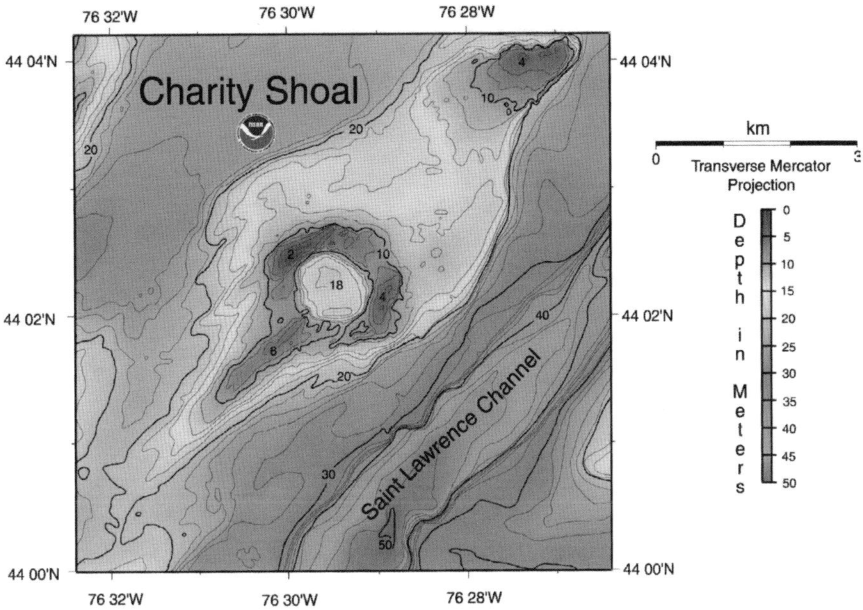

Charity Shoal, believed to be an eroded meteorite impact site, is similar in size and shape to the Barringer Crater in Arizona. It is a little over a mile in diameter. *Lake Ontario chart number seventy-six.*

chart near it. Such anomalies would have affected the accuracy of ships' compasses through the years and could well have contributed to some of the groundings and wrecks that have occurred on Charity Shoal.

In *Gateway to Oblivion: The Great Lakes Bermuda Triangle*, author Hugh Cochrane writes that the area is subject to the influences of the paranormal Marysburg Vortex. Science tells us that impact craters are often associated with magnetic anomalies caused by the massive shock of the meteor hitting the bedrock. Either way, uncharitable Charity Shoal is a place for the wise mariner to avoid. Today, it is well marked by a prominent navigational beacon.

Three large south-shore bays have Sodus in their names. Great Sodus, Little Sodus and Blind Sodus lie within ten miles of one another. Great Sodus is by far the largest. Blind Sodus has never had a permanent channel and remains closed off from the lake by a barrier bar of gravel most of the time. Little Sodus is often called Fair Haven Bay to avoid being confused with the other two. The village of Fair Haven stands at the south end of Little Sodus Bay. Today, local residents like to proclaim that their small, seasonal resort town and its wide, protected warm-water anchorage is one *e* away

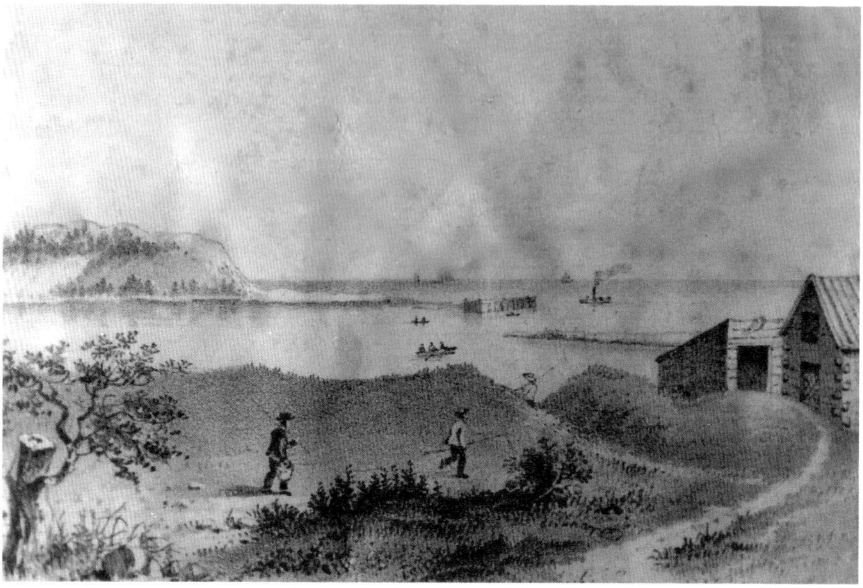

A view of Fair Haven Bay from its northeastern corner in pre-railroad days, here labeled as Ontario Bay. *Sterling Historical Society.*

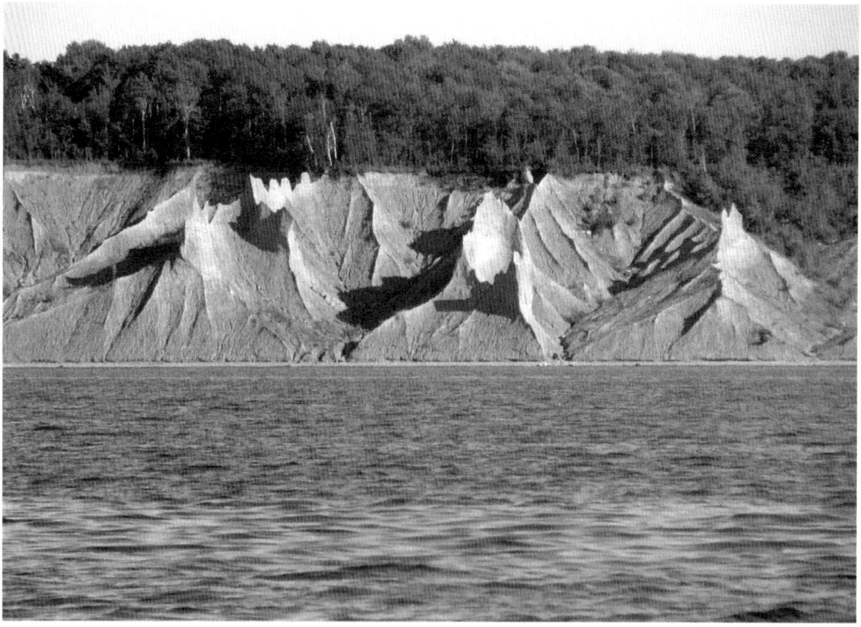

Veins of erosion-resistant clay create the chimneys of this landmark bluff on the lake's south shore. *Author's collection.*

from heaven. Once, it was a bustling commercial harbor, where cargoes of coal, grain and lumber were shipped to and from Canada. However, before the Civil War, the economy stalled here for lack of a connecting rail line to distant markets for cargoes. In a bid to raise interest in building a rail line, boosters in the hamlet of Little Sodus removed the demeaning "little" by officially changing their town's name to Fair Haven. They didn't want to sound like an inconsequential backwater as they tried to raise financing. The local businesses and real estate speculators also attempted, with little luck, to rename their protected anchorage "Ontario Bay." By 1852, a letter from the United States postmaster general had made the use of the name "Fair Haven" for the town official. Though many people refer to the bay as Fair Haven Bay, it remains Little Sodus on the charts.

One of the most prominent landmarks along the lake's south shore between Rochester and Oswego is a large eroding clay bluff called Chimney Bluffs. It was once simply called the Chimneys and is the eroded end of an ice age drumlin hill. (Many of the area's larger drumlins have names. I once lived next to Whiskey Hill, named for an illegal still. Gobbler's Knob is another lofty spot about five miles west of Whiskey Hill.) The Chimneys got its name because of the heavily sculpted ridges and spires that loom above the bluff face.

Drumlins (derived from Gaelic, meaning "mound" or "little ridge") are piles of glacial till dumped when the ice melted. They were then shaped into elongated hills by the flow of a successive glacier's movement. In the lake region, they are generally oriented roughly north–south and are grouped across a considerable part of central New York. The group, or "swarm," of drumlin hills found south of Lake Ontario is one of several such groups around the Great Lakes. Seen from the air, they look a bit like a school of streamlined fish all swimming northward and all of similar size and orientation.

However, they aren't uniform inside. Veins and layers of sand and different kinds of clay lie within them. Some deposits of clay resist erosion to form large pedestals and chimney-like structures on several of the eroding drumlin ends on the lakeshore. A similar big bluff on the Canadian side of the lake (which is not a drumlin) is sometimes called Cathedral Bluffs. Like the Chimneys, it, too, has striking high-relief ridges that presumably resembled the flying buttresses of a cathedral to some early navigator.

Several of the south-shore bluffs have names that are rather dull, as they simply recall past landowners—Sitts, Scotts, McIntyre and Brown's Bluffs among them. One near my house is the "Bean Field Bluff." It's been fifty years or more since any beans grew there, but the name persists.

Just west of Sodus Bay is another prominent high point of land much like the Devil's Nose. Today, it's called Freedom Hill. It once had a less politically correct moniker because of the small settlement of free blacks who lived along Maxwell Creek immediately east of it. These hardy souls sheltered runaway slaves and conveyed them to the lakeshore or to the small bay formed by Maxwell Creek beside the headland, where they were picked up by passing boats and spirited away to freedom in Canada. Local lore mentions one sympathetic schooner captain, George Garlock, and his little two-master, suggestively named *Free Trader*, as being a collaborator. Just down the lake at neighboring Little Sodus Bay, another small vessel, the *Wide Awake*, named for the radical abolitionist wing of the Republican Party, is also said to have ferried slaves north. (See chapter five for more on the underground railroad and Lake Ontario.)

A few miles inland from the present-day south coast of Lake Ontario lies a prominent landmark, called by one writer the longest main street in America. Ridge Road, the wave-built way—as popular twentieth-century upstate author Arch Merrill termed it in his book *The Ridge*—runs from Lewiston to Sodus Bay. It marks the shoreline of prehistoric Lake Iroquois and was an early natural route first for the Native Americans and later for soldiers and settlers moving east and west. Once the border between Canada and the United States was established and U.S. settlement began, a string of towns formed along the Ridge Road, many of them associated with fall lines for north-flowing streams. A sudden drop in the streambed could provide the hydropower for a sawmill, and in those times, a good mill site was often the beginning of a town. Parts of the Ridge are now old Route 104. It dies out east of Sodus Bay, but along some stretches, as between Williamson and Ontario in Wayne County, it's quite prominent and looks like a large version of the berm cast up along the lake's gravel beaches today after a big blow.

South Point, Long Point, Sand and Stony Point, Smokey Point, Fairbanks Point (named for the family that owned it), Nine Mile Point (of which Lake Ontario has several), Thirty Mile Point—the old schooner captains and commercial fishermen knew them all and many more. Their names evoke a slower-paced time when there was ample opportunity while waiting for the wind to study the shoreline. Landmarks in a world with few lighthouses and buoys and no GPS were vital to the art of piloting along a coast. Today's mariner, speeding along at fifty knots in a high-powered cruiser, hardly has time to notice a headland, bluff face or a small bay, assuming he or she ever looks up from the chart plotter to check on the surroundings.

Names Afloat

The Lucky and the Less Fortunate

Many landmarks got their names through some casual association or a simple but memorable event. But ship and boat names are another matter. In years past, mariners selected names for their vessels with care, for a poorly chosen name could have great influence on the ship's fortune. Ship and pleasure boat names even today are associated with little understood but nonetheless potent powers that may influence Lady Luck and the gods of wind and water. Those who venture forth on the lake know that they sail on sometimes dangerous waters, and to this day, many yacht owners believe changing a boat's name will bring bad luck. A few years ago, an elaborate set of precautions and rituals for renaming a boat was making its way around Internet chat rooms and sailing group boards, proving even those who sail for pleasure on gentle summer seas feel it's prudent to be safe rather than sorry about this matter of luck.

The trick to successfully renaming a yacht is to first remove all signs and traces of the boat's old name. She must be "cleansed" before rechristening. This cleansing includes a request to King Neptune to delete the former name from his records. After this request, which has to be made aloud, the boat is given her new name according to standard christening procedure. The superstitious and traditionalist skipper will baptize the boat with a bottle of bubbly after declaring the new name. The less traditional and extravagant may content themselves with pouring a dollop from a can of beer over the side and drinking the rest. Every christening must include a libation of some sort, though.

I've been involved with a half dozen sailboats over the years, two of which had their names changed during my association with them. My first two boats came into my possession with names that I deemed perfectly acceptable so were left unchanged. Both served extremely well for seventeen and twenty years, respectively. Another yacht came into my life with "Rochester NY" on her transom and no indication of a name anywhere, there or elsewhere aboard. It was thus simple enough to give it a new name. The deed was done with appropriate use of a six-pack of beer, and the boat has worn it well since. However, there was one yacht that I failed to rename according to correct protocol.

The boat had been called *Restless*. I didn't care for the moniker and peeled the vinyl letters off. However, the name remained clearly visible on the boat's transom, outlined by grime around where the letters had been. I renamed her but never got around to actually putting the new name on. Nor did I ever make the required alcoholic offering to Neptune. After two years, I sold the boat, sustaining a severe financial loss in the process. Then a few months later, the hapless, and still nameless, yacht was dismasted in a squall. So perhaps there is good reason to follow proper renaming procedure.

Another renamed sloop from my homeport also had a spell of hard luck. She had been damaged in an East Coast hurricane and then brought up to Lake Ontario by a bargain hunter, where she ended up sitting forlornly in his yard for years, grimy, mildewed and disassembled. Her original name, *Patricia*, had been altered to *Travis McGee*, the fictional sleuth and skipper of the yacht *Busted Flush*. At long last, however, the busted and beached sloop changed owners (and names) once again. Although her new owner got her operational, the boat then suffered through a divorce and the indignity of having a storage building collapse on her.

Although it may not impact a boat's luck one way or the other, traditionalists take a dim view of names that demean the vessel or somehow trivialize the whole honorable tradition of naming a boat. *Beer Chaser* and *Addicted*, for example, seem a bit borderline, though the latter is at least an honest assessment of the attitude some of us have when it comes to boating. Most combinations of owner names and initials, while not exactly unlucky, often seem unfortunate, and I despise names like *Trophy Nuts* or *Happy Hooker* seen on fishing boat transoms. Cruisers with names like *Nauty Girl*, the *Office* or *Phartzy* also would seem to tempt the gods of fortune.

Tradition also says a name should never scorn or belittle the elements or issue any sort of challenge to them. A haughty or arrogant ship's name sooner or later always seems to bring trouble. There once was a British battle ship named the *Great Harry*. She ran into ill luck from the start and eventually sank with a terrible loss of life. The *Great Eastern* was another unlucky ship, and we all know what happened to the proud, mighty and unsinkable *Titanic*.

Lake Ontario's working ships of the nineteenth century steered clear for the most part of presumptuous names. A goodly number were named after girlfriends or female family members—*Sally Ann, Diana, Sophia, Julia*—or for some sort of geographic feature, such as a port they often called on. *Niagara, Vandalia* (named for the then capital of Illinois), *Oswego Trader, Sloop Genesee* and *Chicago* were examples of "geographic" names. Then, there were a number of Lake Ontario schooners that were named for creatures somehow associated with the lake or with water in general, a custom followed to this day by some yachtsmen of higher sensibilities and better-developed aesthetics.

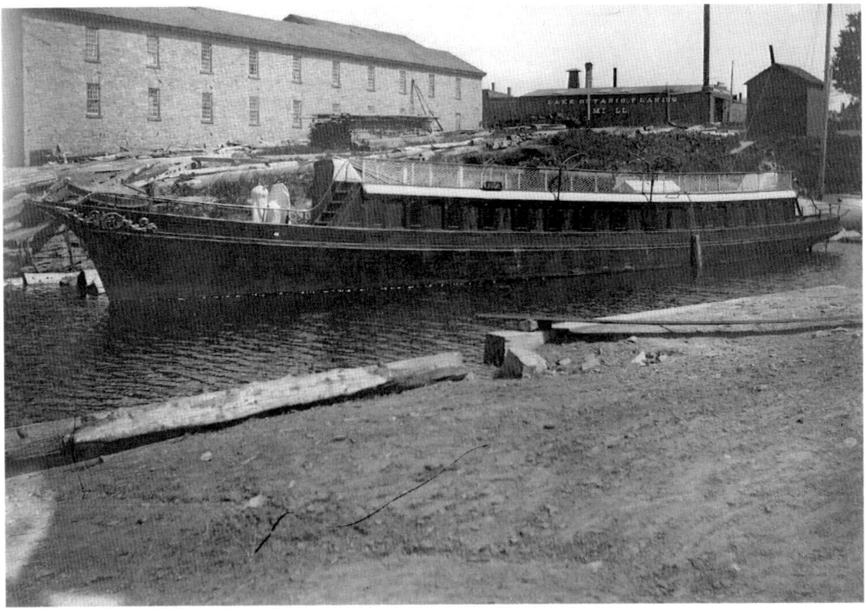

Oswego-built *Aida*, named for the Ethiopian princess of Verdi's opera that premiered shortly before its launch, typifies the classic traditions of nineteenth-century yacht names. *Author's collection.*

Several schooners were given the names of fleet-winged birds, such as the schooner *Wood Duck*, the little sloop *Black Duck* or the schooner *Gannet*. The Canadian schooner *Grampus* went ashore in Oswego below Fort Ontario, and the cove where she was wrecked became known as Grampus Bay.

In modern times, many sailing yachts have also been named for creatures associated with the air or water. A quick sampling includes *Osprey*, *Petrel*, *Oakalee* (the onomatopoeic call of the redwing black bird, a common resident of lake shore marshes), *Dove* and *Puffin*. Nineteenth-century sailors were more familiar with classical literature and mythology than are today's boat owners. Many of their vessels bore names from these sources—*Thisbe*, *Phoebe* and *Ariel* being three Lake Ontario yacht names of yore that come to mind.

Unfortunately, these days an increasing number of yacht names reflect the owner's ego, occupation or preoccupation with boat payments: *Empty Pockets*, *Piggy Bank* and, for the budget boater, *Last Month's Rent*. Still, the practice is somewhat in keeping with the tradition from the nineteenth century of naming commerce carriers for the financier's favorite daughter or for the company that most commonly provided cargoes for it. And then there are

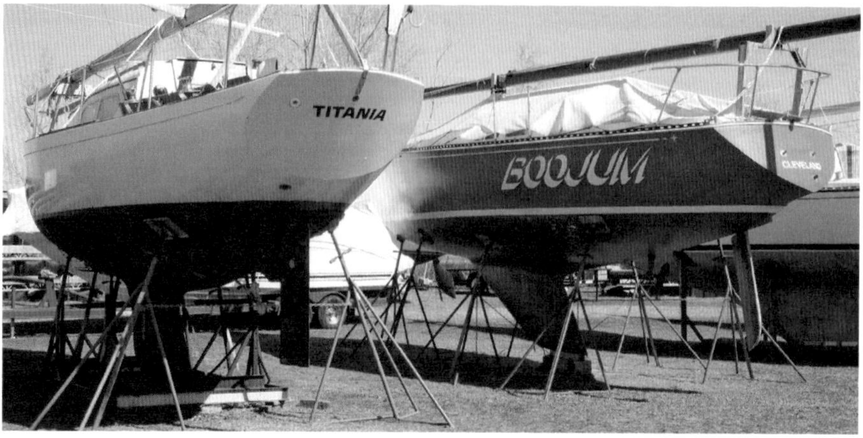

Titania, from Shakespeare's *A Midsummer Night's Dream*, and *Boojum*, from Lewis Caroll's poem the "Hunting of the Snark," follow a tradition of being named for literary characters. *Author's collection.*

the good ships *Enigma* and *Incomprehensible*, presumably owned by thrifty do-it-yourself owners.

Sailors have long believed certain ships are particularly lucky or unlucky. Van Cleve mentions one such vessel that seemed prone to mishaps, the schooner *Frank Pierce*. She ran ashore at Braddock's Bay late one fall and was pushed up the beach so far that she stayed there, protected by ice, all winter. A few years later, she went aground again near Port Credit, this time with a load of iron. Then in 1856, she was found afloat and deserted, loaded with lumber and completely waterlogged. She had been abandoned by the crew, who had piled into the boats in such haste that they left the schooner with some sails still raised.

Another Lake Ontario schooner that was unquestionably unlucky was the *Caroline Ely Simpson*. She was launched in 1858 on the Genesee River and named for her owner's deceased infant daughter who had died in 1852. In 1859, the *Simpson*'s owner sent the schooner down the St. Lawrence, where she picked up a cargo of lumber for Ireland. Apparently business was not good on the lakes, and Simpson hoped to sell his ship abroad.

The schooner had a rough passage on the North Atlantic, however, suffering some damage and putting into port waterlogged and held afloat only by her cargo of Canadian timber. She wasn't exactly in prime condition, so the owner, rather than selling at a huge loss, patched the *Simpson* up and sent her off with a cargo of coal for the West Indies. Somehow the coal got wet and caught fire. The *Simpson* once again barely escaped destruction. She limped into port, was cleaned up and patched and sent off with another load of lumber for Europe.

However, once again the vessel began to leak. A contemporary news account said the crew cut away the spars to keep the ship from capsizing, but this time, she would not be denied. She made her final dive, taking the captain with her, just three years after her launch. The boat never turned a profit, was uninsured and, concluded the 1861 news story, "would seem to have been better for her owner, we presume, if the boat had sunk in Lake Ontario."

Perhaps the *Simpson* is an example of the power of names. It may have been unwise to name the vessel for a deceased child. Or it may be that the *Simpson*'s owner overlooked setting an auspicious date for the launch. Ship launches a century ago were generally accompanied by a number of precautions and rituals to ensure good luck. Wednesday was supposed to be a good day for a launch, and morning was better than afternoon. To this day, skippers still place a silver coin under their yachts' masts to ensure luck when they are put in place for the season.

CHAPTER 4

A FEW LAKESHORE LEGENDS

The "Sprite," a legend of Sodus Bay, was originally written in verse by Mrs. B.C. Rude and published in 1900 in *Two Legends: A Souvenir of Sodus Bay*. (You can read the original online at archive.org.) Two generations before it was written, a veritable pandemic of spiritualism swept the countryside. The Fox sisters of Hydesville, a few miles south of Sodus Bay, had whipped up a frenzy of passion and controversy with their séances and communications with the dead. This was also a time of religious revivalism of such a fever pitch that the region became known as the burned-over district. Perhaps this preoccupation with spirits and unknown mysteries got a boost from the terrifying beauty of a November night in 1833 a few years before this story is said to have happened. That night, a meteor storm occurred, during which a Niagara Falls witness wrote, "Thousands of stars came in waves and a succession of brilliant fireballs terrified many."

Captain Hosea Rogers, who saw the meteor shower while sailing his schooner down the lake, wrote:

> *I shall never forget my last voyage that season. By ten o'clock we had our hatches battened down and every loose thing on deck was swept overboard. The gale became terrific, and we hardly expected to outlive it. Suddenly there was a cry that the heavens were falling as the great dome above us was filled with shooting stars. We had no intimation of the auroral display and coming as it did at an hour when every nerve was strained and every sense alive to the dangers of the elements, the scene was particularly impressive.*

> *The shower lasted several hours, if I remember correctly...We battled with the elements and watched the unprecedented fall of stars until the morning of the 13th when daylight ended the wonderful display.*

Did this swarm of falling stars help stimulate the belief in mysteries and visions referred to below? Ganargua's ghost, mentioned at the end, was supposedly a Seneca chief.

The Sprite

Once, there lived on the shore of Lake Ontario near Sodus Bay a miserly old man named Dobbs and his fair and gentle wife. Their home stood on the shore just west of Sodus Bay, overlooking its entrance channel. It was not a happy home. Dobbs, a cold and distant man, cared only for his gold. However, after death took his wife's sister, her child, a little girl named Katherine, was sent to the Dobbs household to live. The child brought a ray of warmth into that dark, barren home, and Dobbs's wife lavished all her frustrated love and mothering on her niece.

The little girl had grown into a comely, slender maid whose eyes were the color of the lake's distant waters on a sunny day and whose hair gleamed black and lustrous when illness and then death visited the household and claimed her foster mother. Now, the young woman was left unloved and alone, taking her meager meals in silence at the frugal table with Dobbs before climbing the stairs with a candle to her unheated bedroom. Like Dobbs, she, too, shunned society and turned inward to dwell in a shadowy world peopled with memories of the dead. One of her few contacts with the wider world was a neighbor youth, young Morris, the lighthouse keeper's son. He came with a shy smile now and then to offer fresh-caught perch to the household.

Katherine, they say, had a bit of the "sight," and lying in her narrow bed in the long nights of winter, she often heard rapping and tapping sounding loudly throughout the house. She wondered whether it was rats or squirrels in the wall or something else causing the noises. And when a cold chill passed over her, she questioned if it was only a draft from the rattling window. As she lay sleepless with the October wind whimpering and whining outside, she would watch the flash of the Sodus light gleaming pale on the bedroom wall opposite the window. She found comfort in its silent constancy and in knowing its guardian keeper stood vigil over the entrance to the bay each night.

The lighthouse then stood on the end of the jetty that jutted far out into the lake, and both the wooden light tower and its keeper were a bit worse for wear. That fall, after Katherine's aunt died, the old man who had watched the light for nearly fifty years gave up the post and turned the key to the tower over to his son, Morris: "My boy, you know not fear nor wrong, my limbs are failing yours are strong. I now resign to you this trust, oh boy of mine."

Only a day or two later, a November gale blew up, and young Morris had to make his way out to the light using the iron catwalk suspended above the jetty. He went out in late afternoon, before the waves built up enough to wash over the jetty. Out over the lake, the sky was a lead gray and the wind cut cold and strong from the northwest. Already surf crashed on the shore, and spray flew across the jetty and catwalk in clouds of white.

Morris picked his way out over the slippery walkway prepared to spend the night (and the next day, also, if need be) staying on watch in the tower. By dark, the catwalk would be too wave swept for safe passage.

That evening, Katherine, in the house on the hill, heard the wild boom and roar of the surf over the wind's bass bluster through the trees. It was a night when old Ontario looked truly like an inland sea. As she sat, she heard someone suddenly cry out, "The pier! The light! The pier, I say!" This was no voiceless rapping of an enigmatic ambiguous spirit. This was a direct warning. She jumped up, and as she turned toward the window to look out, a vision formed sharply in her mind of the twisted splintered wooden light tower being swept off the pier by an immense wave. Her neighbor, young Morris, was in that tower.

Katherine seized a shawl from its peg by the door and bolted out of the house. She ran with all her might down the hill and then stood at the end of the pier. She could feel the entire structure quiver and shake with the blows of massive waves slamming against it. Never had she seen such a storm. She waited, gripping the iron rail, until three waves—waves as big as houses—swept clean over the jetty. Then she ran for her life, sprinting for the tower at the end during the brief lull following the giant seas.

She reached it breathless and jammed herself within the door recess, shouting and pounding on the oaken boards: "Morris, you must leave the light! Get out, Morris!" Morris pulled open the heavy door just as another wave hit, and a tremendous crack of breaking timbers and framing rang out from the tower. No more words were required: stay and die, or run for it and possibly live. They bolted. Scarcely had they made it to shore when another huge breaker, reaching halfway up the tower, smote it such a blow that with a creak and a groan of rending wood it toppled into the channel.

Katherine and Morris looked at each other in horror, and then she whirled and ran again, vanishing into the wind-rent blackness. But Morris's work was not done. The light was gone, but mariners might even now be desperately scanning the blackness ahead of them for its flash of hope and sanctuary in this wild night. Several neighbors had gathered around him, and he turned now to ask with flashing eyes and firm resolve "Who'll plant a light off Charles Point?" One sturdy brave soul, an old but still strong fisherman named Johnny Bell, stepped forward. "Yes Morris lad, I'll tack about. Now come, who will, man or lout?"

They hurried to the fish house where Bell's little skiff lay and rigged her with a scrap of sail. Even the protected waters of the bay leapt under the small boat and slapped hard at her bows as she scudded over to the bluff to plant a light and then tacked back. A second light was placed on the overlooking bank to the west. There was nothing more they could do. Morris retraced his steps upon landing, and in the sand by the jetty, he found a woman's slipper made of red leather.

The storm abated. A new light was hastily rigged on the pier, and life returned to normal. But Morris remembered the maid whose warning he had heeded. One day, he heard Old Dobbs the miser was dead. Katherine promptly abandoned the dreary old house, and nearly before Dobbs was cold in his gave, a mob of neighbors descended on the house convinced that the miser's horde lay buried there. They ransacked the rooms and searched and scattered the pitiful belongings of kitchen and hearth all about the yard. Morris, coming by the next morning, found the mate to the slipper from the beach lying trampled in the mud. So it had been Katherine who had come to him in the night with her warning cry.

Winter passed away as it always does, melting into spring. Katherine razed the old house and put up a new home a short distance from where the first had stood. It seemed that she had known where Dobb's horde was kept and was its heiress, but she still refused the young suitors who now came even more eagerly and frequently to her door. Summer came and with it, another suitor, the awkward youth Morris with his shy smile. He stopped one June morning and invited her to go for a sail with him on Sodus Bay.

The air was limpid, and the clean wind was gentle and steady out of the west. Morris had borrowed Johnny Bell's skiff for the day, and they cast off

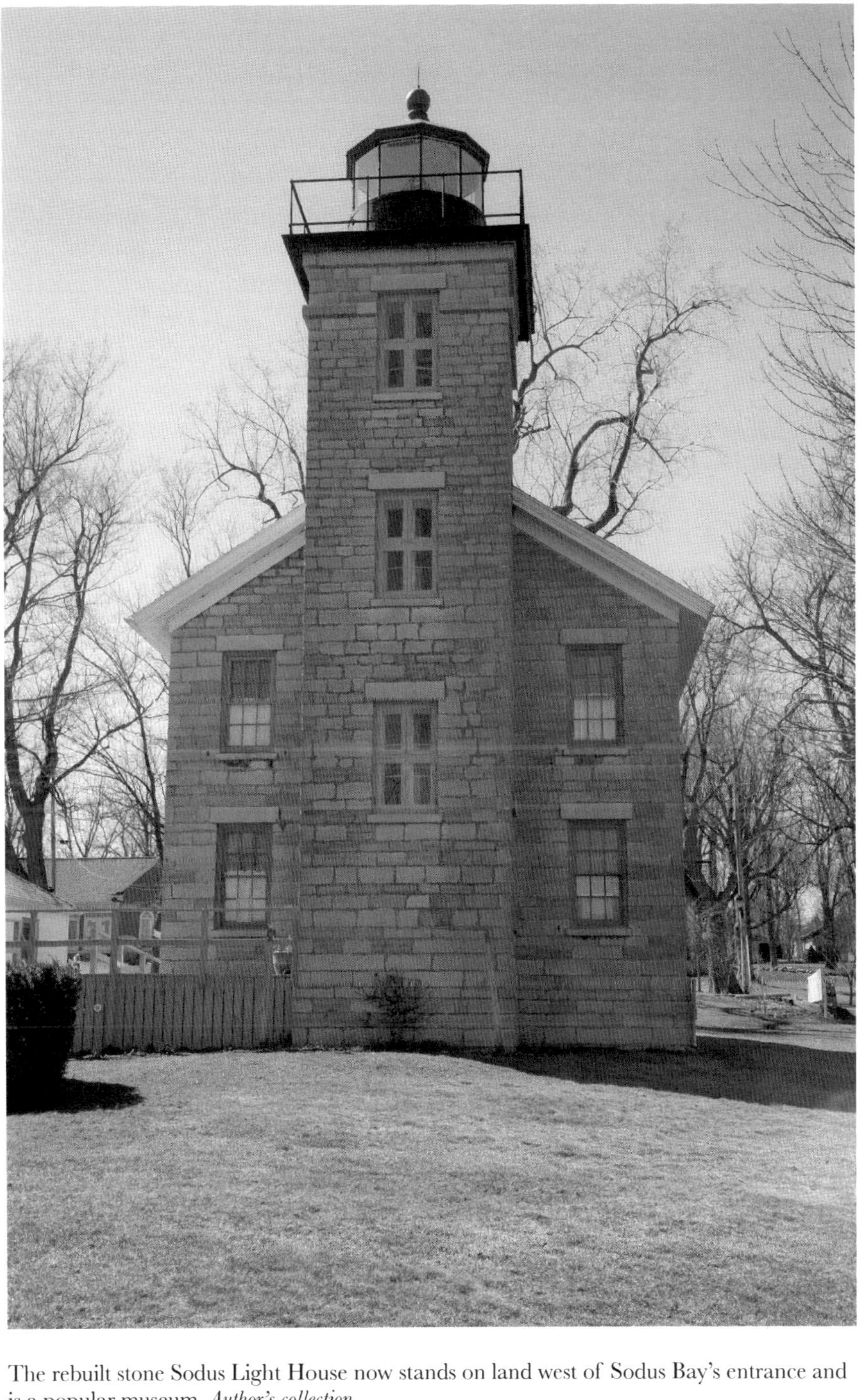

The rebuilt stone Sodus Light House now stands on land west of Sodus Bay's entrance and is a popular museum. *Author's collection.*

to glide across the bay's clear waters. They skimmed over sunlit shallows, past forested slopes, farm fields and summer cottages, before ducking behind the Islands of Arran and Islay. Here in the lea where the cool wind off the lake gave way to early summer's warmth, Morris and Katherine exchanged a long look, then a lingering kiss, and love flowed between them.

Then, as now, stories get around. It was a grand wedding. Half the town turned out for it, and the story of Katherine's warning was oft repeated, losing nothing in the telling: "And ne'er was sweeter service said, than that which gave to Morris May a bride upon that holiday." The bride wore a splendid gown, a pair of slightly battered red leather slippers and a smile of pure sunshine that afternoon.

In the years to come, theirs was a house of welcome and warmth. Friends and neighbors gathered there, and stories, laughter and songs echoed forth over the lake on summer evenings. Still, particularly on frosty November evenings, it was said, sometimes a strange glimmer or a wisp of fog could be seen over the cellar hole where Dobb's house had once stood. Some say it's Ganargua's ghost, but the identity of the guardian spirit that warned Katherine of Morris's peril remains forever a mystery.

Indian Lore

No account of Lake Ontario shoreline lore would be complete without a few Indian legends, a number of which feature water in one form or another. The People of the Longhouse had several versions of the Creation Story featuring various aquatic creatures. Here's a short rendering of one.

The story goes that Awehai, First Woman, became part of a lover's triangle, and her jilted husband, infuriated, tore up the tree that was at the center of the world. He then threw Awehai into the hole. As she fell, Awehai reached out and seized the life around her. She gathered seeds and plants and several small animals, including beaver, otter, frog and toad. As she neared the lake's surface, birds flew to the spot and cushioned her landing with their wings.

After floating about for a while, Awehai eventually washed up on the great turtle's back, and the small but adept swimming animals she had brought along hurried about gathering clods of dirt from the great world tree's roots. (Another version of the tale has a humble little muskrat diving to the bottom of the lake to bring up a bit of mud after all the other animals had tried and

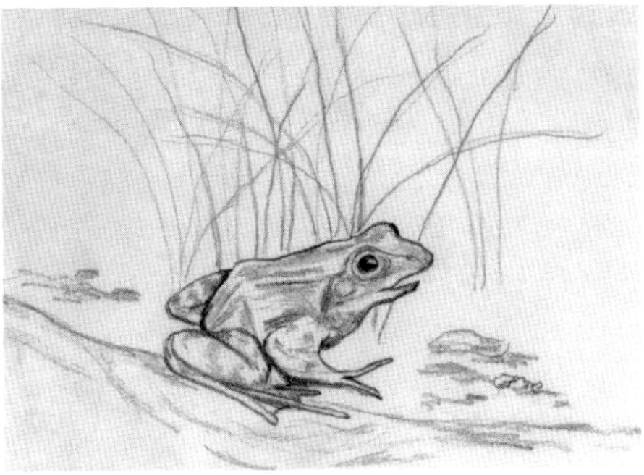

Noisgwais, the frog of Iroquois stories. *Artwork by Pat Cooper.*

failed to find some solid earth.) This dirt was then formed into an island that became our earth floating in an unthinkably vast primeval lake. Awehai then scattered the seeds and plants she'd managed to grab during her fall. Soon earth was green and good and filled with life.

History records that our upstate New York tribes used dugout or elm bark and frame canoes to navigate both Lake Ontario and the inland Finger Lakes. They lacked access to the fine big birch trees that the Hurons in Canada used to make their famous lightweight but strong birch bark canoes. The Iroquois, not surprisingly, never attained a mastery of the water equal to that of some tribes, and a number of their legends suggest a certain unease with and healthy respect for larger bodies of water.

Several legends tell of heroes vanquishing large, dangerous or otherwise unsettling creatures such as a giant leech, a giant grub or a huge serpent found at the bottom of a lake or pond. And then there are references to *Jijogweh,* the witch water gull, a night-flying bird that thirsted for blood and possessed poison breath. If this creature dropped a feather, blood appeared and destroyed whatever life it touched.

Giant serpents figure in a number of upstate Indian legends, including that of Bare Hill on the east side of Canandaigua Lake. When that monster was destroyed, its blood gave rise to all the snakes of the forests and grasslands of today. A Seneca legend tells of two tribes of serpents or underwater creatures, also referred to as underwater people, named the Ongwiias and the slightly less evil Jodikwa. These mythical aquatic creatures were the sworn enemy of the Indian demigod Heno, the Great Thunderer. Heno pursued these water creatures relentlessly for they sometimes had been known to emerge from the water and cast spells on children to coax them into the deadly cold depths. Heno would harass the serpent people by throwing lightning bolts at them until they swam down into the depths of the lake for refuge. A popular legend about the Great Thunderer concerns his adopted son, the Thunder Boy.

One day Heno, who was also in charge of bringing rain to the land, sent a bit too much rain down. The land became flooded, and as the floodwaters rose, Heno sent down one of his assistants to help the Senecas. As this spirit

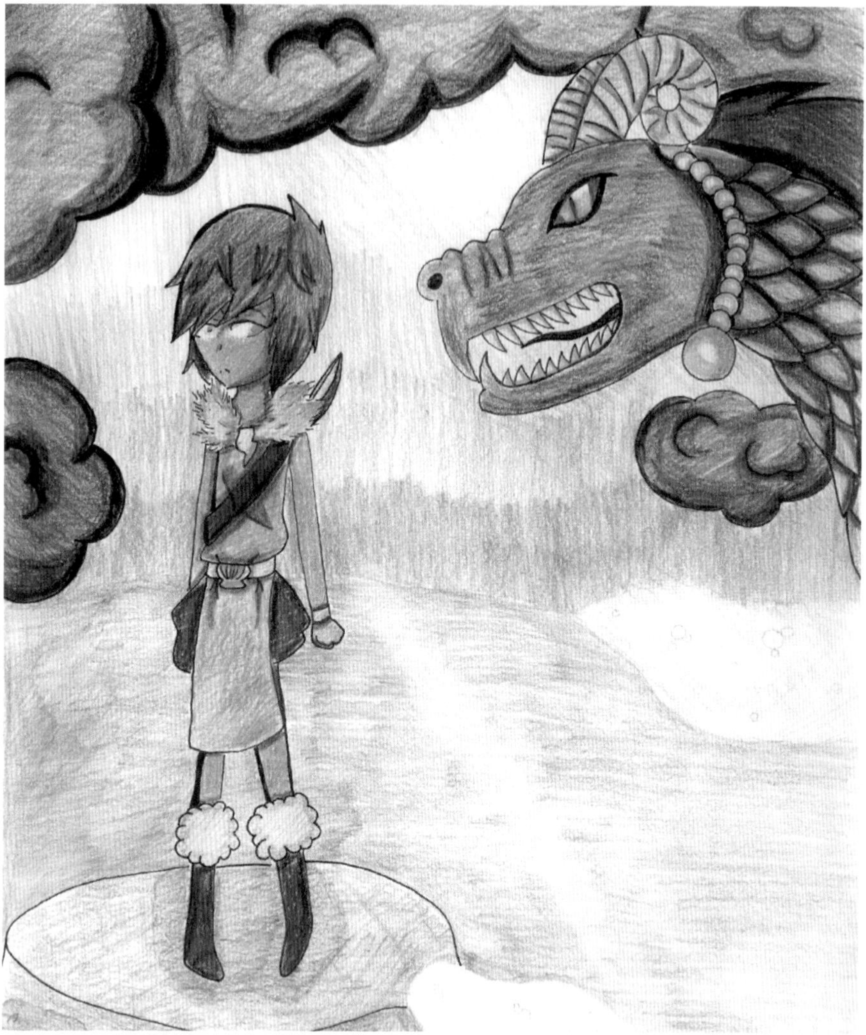

Gunnodoyah and the serpent. *By Katie Dawson.*

servant passed over one town, he heard a child's cry. It was a little boy named Gunnodoyah, adrift in the flood, orphaned and alone. The spirit took up the little boy and carried him back to Heno's house in the clouds. Heno then adopted him and trained him in the ways of a thunder hunter.

At this time, there dwelt a monster in the depths of Lake Ontario. This great serpent was often seen by the people, and it destroyed the salmon and trout they sought for food. Gunnodoyah, now a sturdy young lad, retained his earthly form, so Heno gave him a strong bow and arrows and told him,

"You must follow the storms and find and kill the troublesome lake serpent." Gunnodoyah followed the black clouds to the lake's shore. There, he searched and waited until at last he saw the monster rise to the surface. He aimed his arrow but missed his mark, and the creature disappeared beneath the lake. Twice more, Gunnodoyah saw the serpent, and twice more his arrows failed to strike it.

At last, there came a particularly powerful storm. The boy again followed the wind and clouds, and this time, he waded right into the lake to meet the snake. Again he drew his bowstring back. Instead of vanishing, the huge serpent spoke to him: "Come near." It said it was not afraid of either Gunnodoyah or his adopted father, Heno the Great Thunderer. It then offered the boy a truce: "Come with me to my home under the lake. I will teach you all the secrets of the water world, and you will be as powerful as I." Gunnodoyah's answer was to aim his arrow and draw back his bowstring. It snapped. The arrow fell harmlessly into the water, and the serpent immediately seized the boy and swallowed him.

Heno, far away and asleep in his cloud home, was awakened by a dream of Gunnodoyah's mishap. Heno sent forth his six servant spirits who dived into the water and swam down to the serpent's cave. They subdued the monster and took it up to Heno, who then killed it and cut it open to pull Gunnodoyah out alive.

But in the years to come, Senecas, on viewing the lake's big rollers crashing onto the shore, would note that the serpent was still down there "twisting the water." And when the summer lightning forks and flashes across the sky or stabs down into the water, they say Gunnodoyah the Thunder Boy is still chasing the lake serpent.

One of the most popular and enduring First Nation tales is that of the Maid of the Mist, also known as Lelawala. Long ago, the peaceful tribe of the Ongiaras lived beside the Niagara River. For an unknown reason, people were dying, and it was believed that the tribe must appease the Thunder God Heno, who lived with his two sons in a cave behind the falls. At first, the tribe sent canoes laden with fruit flowers and game over the falls, but the dying continued. The people then began to sacrifice the most beautiful maiden of the tribe, selected once a year during a ceremonial feast. One year, Lelawala, daughter of Chief Eagle Eye, was chosen.

On the appointed day, Lelawala appeared on the riverbank above the falls, wearing a white doeskin robe with a wreath of woodland flowers in her hair. She stepped into a white birch bark canoe and plunged over the falls to her death. Her father, heartbroken, leapt into his canoe and followed her. Heno's two sons caught Lelawala in their arms, and each desired her. She promised to accept the one who told her what evil was killing her people. The younger brother told her of a giant water snake that lay at the bottom of the river. Once a year, the monster snake grew hungry and, at night, entered the village and poisoned the water. The snake then devoured the dead.

Lelawala returned to the village and told her people they must destroy the serpent. Indian braves mortally wounded the snake on its next yearly visit to the village. Drifting down the river to its lair on the river, the damaged snake caught its head on one side of the river and its tail on the other, forming a semicircle that became the brink of the Horseshoe Falls. There, it remains, petrified in stone to this day. Lelawala returned to the cave of the God Heno, where she reigns as the Maid of the Mist.

CHAPTER 5

FREE TRADE, SMUGGLING AND DARK DEEDS ON THE BORDER

Smuggling has been going on between the north and south shores of Lake Ontario for as long as trade and taxes have existed here. As soon as the Jay Treaty fixed the geographic border between the United States and Canada in 1796, people began moving to the south shore of the lake, clearing land and settling on farms and in towns. With them came trade. The north side of the lake had a head start on settlement as the British had offered land there to a number of Loyalist refugees from the colonies during the Revolutionary War. Prince Edward County, directly across the lake from the Sodus-Rochester stretch of shore, was one of the first coastal areas to be settled. Soon, pioneering Yanks were trading potash, salt and hardwoods for imports like tea and manufactured goods. Because of high American tariffs and duties on these goods, smuggling was widespread, and trying to control it led to the launch of the brig *Oneida*, the first American war ship on the lake.

The *Oneida* seized the schooner *Lord Nelson* two weeks before the War of 1812 began, claiming that the *Nelson* was smuggling. Her owners thought differently. They claimed the *Lord Nelson* had been carrying a perfectly legal cargo of flour and sued for compensation. The schooner was added to the navy's roster and renamed the *Scourge*. The following year, she capsized and took most of her crew with her in a sudden night squall. But her name lived on in the courts long after the War of 1812's conclusion. In 1817, the Americans admitted that they had been wrong, and in 1818, the House passed legislation to compensate the ship's owners. But the Senate killed it.

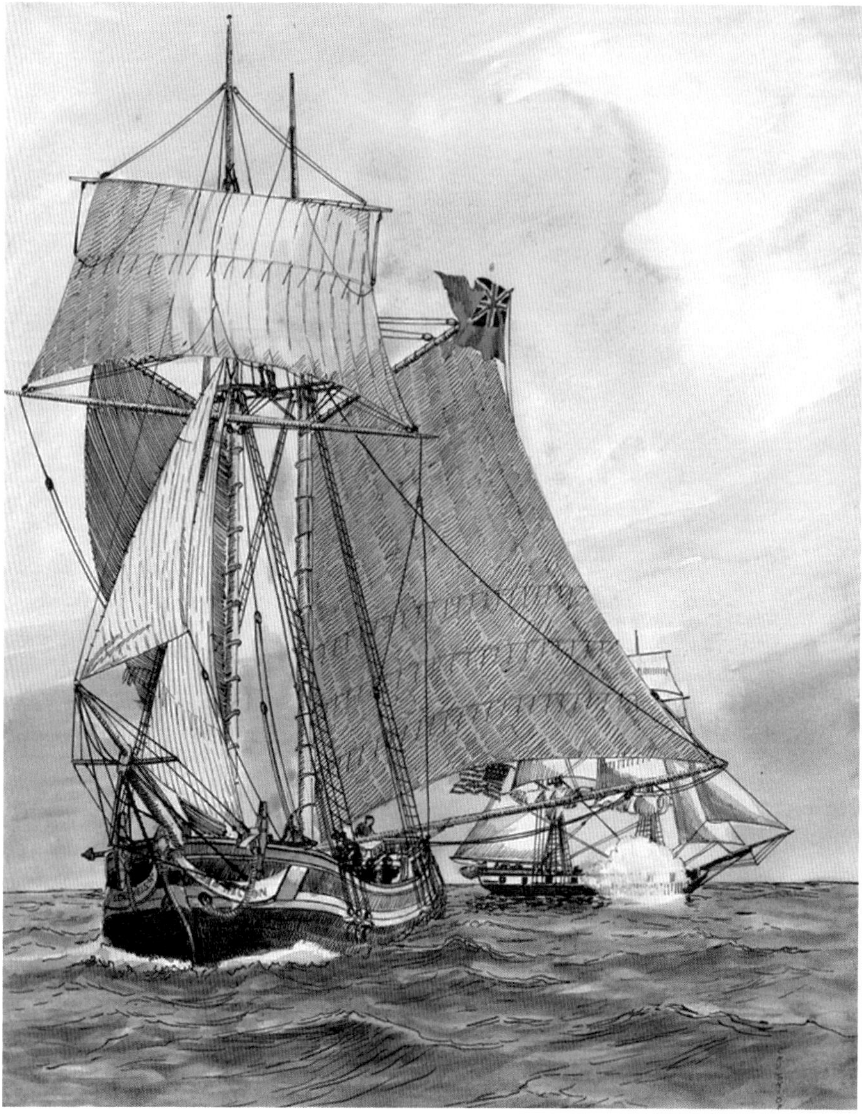

The U.S. brig *Oneida* seized the *Lord Nelson* well before the War of 1812 began. *C.H.J. Snider illustration.*

The family persisted. In 1886, President Cleveland recommended the bill be paid. It wasn't. In 1914, the outstanding "ancient grudge" was included in a treaty. But still no money came. A.D. Crooks, a Toronto lawyer and the grandson of James Crook, the ship owner who originally was awarded

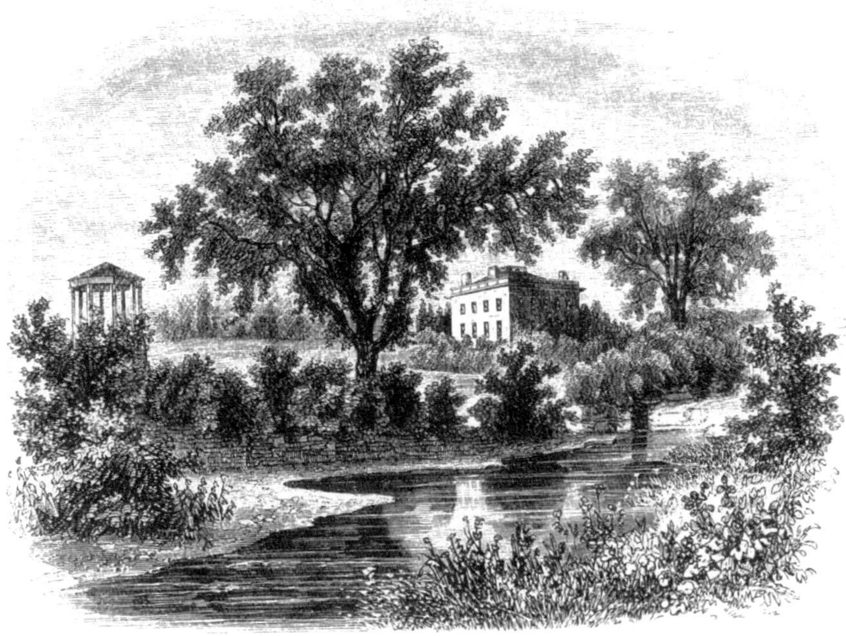

General Brown's mansion built of cut limestone in 1813–14. Possibly some of the money for construction came from smuggled potash. *From* Lossing's Pictorial Field Book of the 1812 War.

the money, went to Washington, and at long last, thirteen years later, the money was paid. It amounted to $23,644.63, the original $5,000 plus simple interest. Historian and retired lawyer Robert Townsend noted that the amount would have been over $1 million had the interest been compounded after 117 years of litigation.

One of the best-known American generals of the War of 1812 was Jacob Brown, a one-time schoolteacher and land speculator who founded Brownsville just west of Watertown. He is remembered for saving the day at Sackets Harbor during a crucial battle. But according to Jon Lattimer's article "Smuggling and Contraband in the War of 1812," before that war, he was also an active and effective smuggler running potash into Canada, where it was used in the manufacture of gun powder. The British were fighting the French at the time and were paying up to three dollars for one hundred pounds of potash in Montreal, a major regional market for the material.

Even after war was declared, the smuggling continued. Colonel Robert Carr, after he arrived in Sackets Harbor in June 1813, wrote: "A trade is clandestinely carried on and a number of villains are engaged in supplying the enemy with flour, pork & salt—by sending out loaded boats to such places as the English can capture them and the men are sent back to report their being captured and plundered—but they are always richer after their losses. It is to be hoped that hemp [the hangman's noose] will come into more general use in this district."

Widespread smuggling continued right through the war. On August 27, 1814, the governor in chief of British North America, Lieutenant General Sir George Prevost, wrote that "two-thirds of the British Army in Canada are, at this Moment, eating Beef provided by American Contractors drawn principally from the States of Vermont and New York while a brigade of artillery recently arrived at Cornwall from southern France was feeding its horses American supplied hay." Near the end of the war, the British built several small warships on Lake Champlain to take on the U.S. fleet, and a key battle, one of the bloodiest of the entire war, ensued. The timber for their masts was supplied by Yankee lumbermen.

After the war, smuggling continued. Luxury goods like tea, silk and other fine fabric items, along with rum and wine, continued to flow across the border. There are tales of small, nimble schooners ducking behind islands and into creeks to evade the law and of shootouts and killings on land, too. And there are stories of ships towing barrels of booze lashed alongside but under water to get them into port. From the Oswego newspaper in 1863 comes this story of a bust made aboard the good ship *Mermaid*:

> *Some time since, Mrs. S. Snoody, keeper of a saloon on the tow-path, in the vicinity of the first* [canal] *lock, in company with Mr. Wm. Tyler, purchased the swift sailing boat* Mermaid, *which craft, with the repairs they put upon her, such as decking over, cabin, &c., necessitated an outlay of about $300. Taking on a cargo at this port consisting of oranges, lemons, &c., the proprietors of the* Mermaid *started on a cruise for Her Majesty's dominions. They visited Belleville, disposed of the cargo and started on their return way of Kingston. At the latter place we understand the return cargo was shipped, consisting of flour casks of "Morton's Proof." Each cask contained from twenty-one to twenty-three gallons—making a total of eighty-five gallons.*

Alas for her crew and owner, the *Mermaid* was caught red-handed by Captain Childs of the Oswego Custom's House as the casks were being unloaded.

Booze went both ways across the lake, depending on local laws and the rise and fall of temperance movements in the United States and Canada.

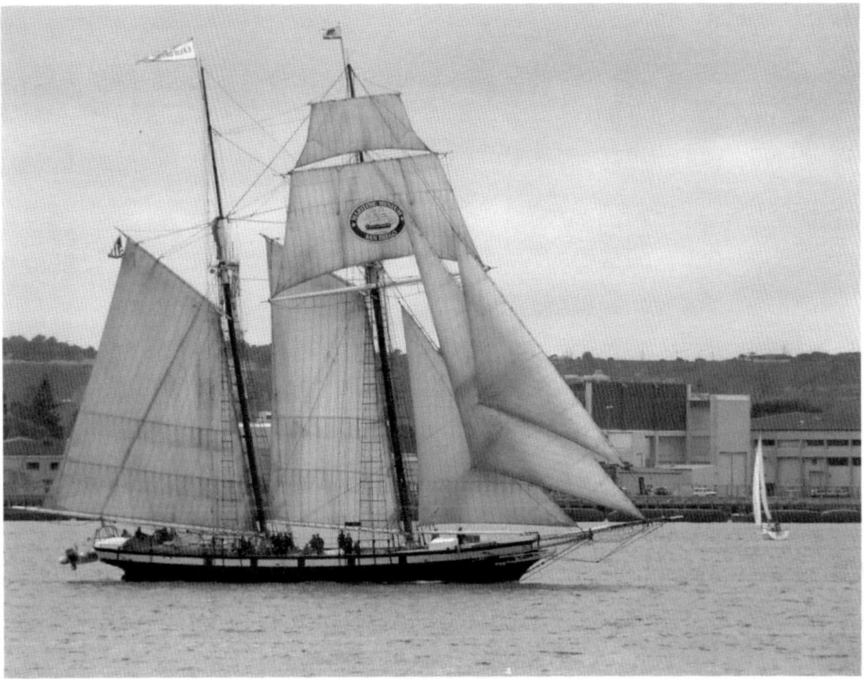

The topsail schooner *Californian* is a replica of an 1847 revenue cutter built to catch smugglers. *Author's collection.*

The well-known Prohibition era (1920–33), during which vast volumes of whiskey and Canadian ale came across Lake Ontario into the United States, has been documented by several authors, including myself. Staggering amounts of money were made during that time. A good haul could easily net the rumrunner $3,000 for a single trip, a year's wages for many workmen back then. An account of the activities of the "King of the Lake Ontario rum runners," Ben Kerr, says that at one time he had three boats hauling booze into the Rochester area and that, when conditions were good, they would make more than one trip a day. Some of the rumrunners used the old trick of using the lake to hide the goods. They would sling fishing nets alongside port and starboard and load them up with cases of booze ballasted with salt bags. If the Coast Guard spotted them, they would cut the load loose. The bags of salt would drag it to the bottom. Then, a few days later, after the salt had dissolved, the rumrunners would return to find the floating cases. However, at least once the trick failed them. On Lake Erie, the story goes, they dumped the load near shore and fled. But the next day, a big

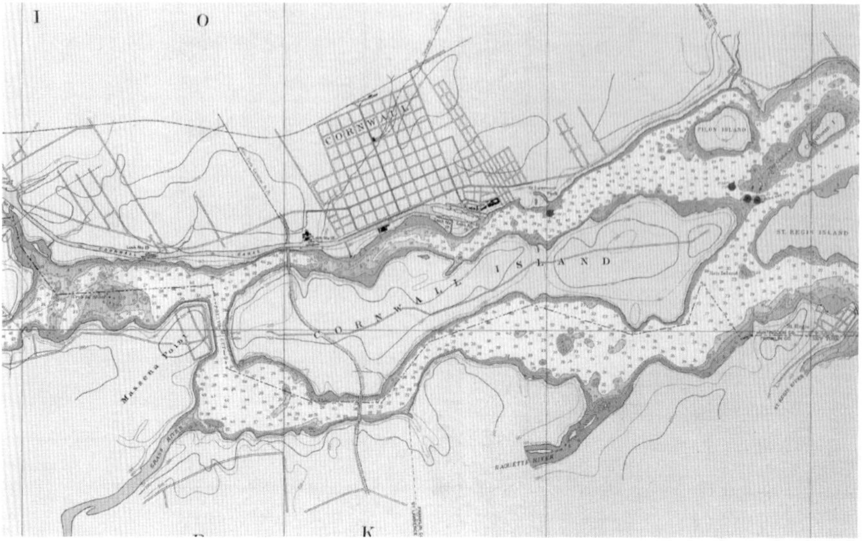

This chart, made prior to the St. Lawrence Seaway, shows the Cornwall area, long a favored smugglers route. *U.S. War Department chart number eleven.*

seiche dropped the lake level and pulled the water away, and there, to the delight of the locals, lay dozens of cases of prize whiskey high and dry on the previously submerged shore. It was a grand day for bottom fishing.

The extreme profits from the booze export trade fueled the rise of organized crime on both sides of the lake, and once Prohibition was lifted, the bosses, dons, kingpins and unscrupulous CEOs of legitimate front companies diversified into opium, heroin, other drugs and guns and kept right on smuggling. In recent years, everything from cigarettes, cheese and disposable diapers to AK-47s and grenade launchers has passed illegally across the U.S. border into Canada. Akwesasne on the St. Lawrence River, where law enforcement must deal with no fewer than four jurisdictions (Ontario, Quebec, New York State and Mohawk), continues to be a hot spot for high-stakes smuggling. Estimates of the value of the illegal trade vary, but it may amount to over $1 billion a year. It's been claimed that a third to half of the cigarettes sold in the Province of Ontario in recent years are contraband. In 2008, according to a news story in the *Toronto Star*, the Royal Canadian Mounted Police (RCMP) seized 1,079,529 cartons of illegal cigarettes at the Cornwall crossing. Profits from illegal smokes are used to finance drug labs that produce synthetics like Ecstasy to send south to U.S. markets. Formerly, the cigarettes came north from low-tax tobacco-producing states like Virginia and the Carolinas. Today, factories on the reservation produce fifty million cigarettes a year using refined tobacco from the south, according to the RCMP as quoted in the news story. Many of these are sold through reservation stores that are tax-free.

Cigarette smuggling has gone on for decades along the St. Lawrence. Like the rumrunners of olden days, smoke smugglers are viewed by a lot of smokers favorably since their efforts make the product so much more affordable. Twenty years ago, a boating friend of mine remembered being tied up at a dock in the St. Lawrence with his sailboat. In the middle of the night, he awoke to the sound of hushed men's voices on the dock. He got up to take a look. A light played over the cabin of his boat, and he ducked down out of the window. Then, as he watched, a powerboat came alongside, and several boxes were transferred to a nearby truck. It looked like a small-scale cigarette deal to him. Since then, U.S. Border Patrol has beefed up its presence along the land-based crossings, which some believe has caused river traffic to increase.

The Niagara Falls border crossings also see their share of smuggling. In early 2013, two trucks were busted at the border with over $3 million of loose tobacco leaf. One was entering with boxes labeled "Recycled Paper," and the other truck's shipping container was full of "Herbal Leaves." Here, and elsewhere also, as guns and cigarettes go north, illegal immigrants and drugs flow south. In one story posted online about traffic on the St. Lawrence, the traffic on one dark night was so heavy that a smoke smuggling boat collided with a man on a jet ski coming south with a load of drugs. It's a year-round trade, as in the winter, when the river freezes, snowmobiles, cars and trucks zip across the ice with the goods.

Enforcement officials say that both Russian and Italian mobs are behind the activity in the Cornwall area. They often hire young runners from the reservation and pay them a few hundred dollars per trip while they make hundreds of thousands behind the scene. With few legitimate jobs in this "rust belt" region, there's no shortage of willing workers who will risk winter ice or gunfire. In 2009, the RCMP beefed up its patrols on the river using a larger Coast Guard catamaran as a base from which its small speedboats chased down the smugglers. Since a runner on a personal watercraft can carry $2 million of ecstasy, it's not hard to see the difficulty that the RCMP faces as it deals with the highly motivated smugglers.

People, like merchandise, have also long passed over the border without official government approval. In the early nineteenth century, many families and individuals passed quietly and easily from one nation to the other. The

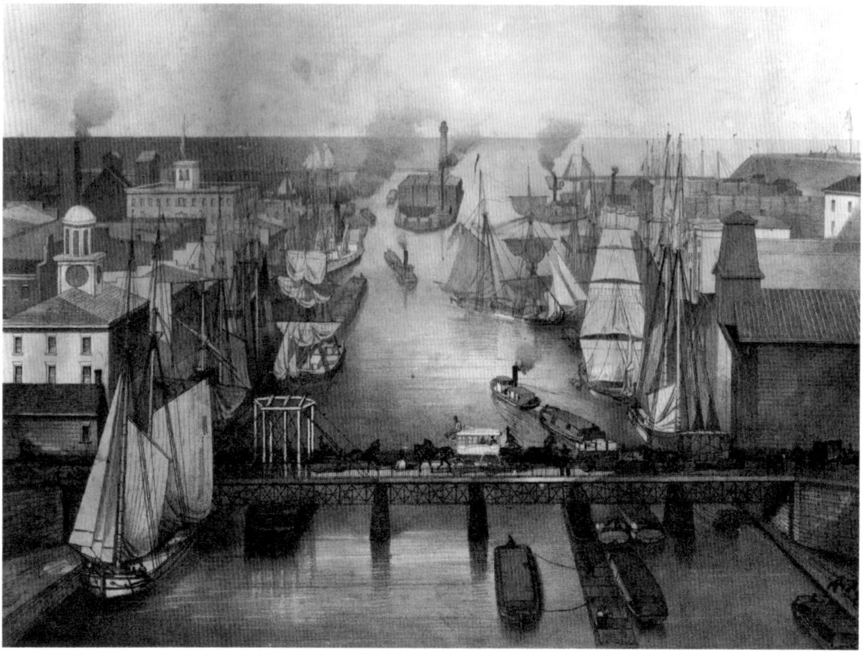

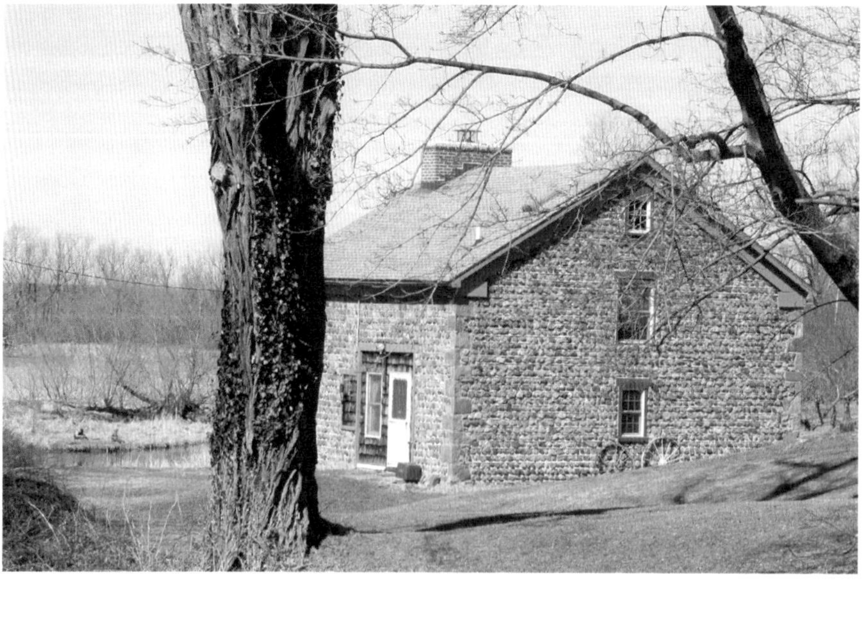

most celebrated illegal movement of humans from the United States to Canada was that of runaway slaves being guided north on the Underground Railroad in the 1840s and '50s. We have no idea how many slaves passed through Great Lakes ports en route to freedom. Few written records of the Underground Railroad exist, and accounts are difficult to verify. It seems likely, however, that hundreds or maybe thousands crossed through the Lake Ontario region on their way to Canada. Oswego's port—where Gerrit Smith, a prominent and wealthy abolitionist from the town of Peterboro near Utica, had interests in shipping and harborfront properties—was a gateway to freedom for many slaves.

Port Ontario, Fair Haven and Pultneyville were also ports with known sympathetic ship captains and ship owners who helped runaways.

Sodus Point and the immediate area harbored several abolitionists who acted as Underground Railroad conductors. A settlement of free blacks lived on the banks of Maxwell Creek, a few miles west of this small lake port. Undoubtedly, they sheltered runaways and helped them on their way, as did the family living in the cobblestone house that still stands there beside Lake Road. Local legend has it that the drumlin hill just west of Maxwell Creek (now known as Freedom Hill) was a landmark used by mariners who picked up runaways off the beach there.

In Sodus Point itself, a man named Jacob Buys was, according to family legend, active in transporting slaves out to waiting schooners in the bay. His house was on North Fitzhugh Street, and a tunnel from it was used to sneak the runaways out to the bay's shore. (At that time, before extensive fill had been placed in low-lying areas, the shore was considerably closer to the house location.) Around 1976, when the town was installing sewers, workers uncovered the tunnel between the house and shoreline. Written evidence of Mr. Buys's political views also exists to support the family story. He is known to have been a member of the Liberty Party, a short-lived abolitionist political group, and he was "read out" of the Sodus Presbyterian Church in 1843 for his outspoken views on slavery.

Opposite, top: Oswego waterfront in the 1850s around the peak of Underground Railroad traffic through this port. *Author's collection.*

Opposite, bottom: This former mill on Maxwell Creek was said to be connected to a nearby house by a tunnel. *Author's collection.*

The Niagara Falls area was also a major crossing for runaways, and a considerable number came up through the Hudson Valley and then were transported west on the Erie Canal to the Buffalo region. Harriet Tubman, one of the most famous conductors of the Underground Railroad, often used the Niagara area as her crossing point. She helped at least seventy people reach freedom and made over a dozen trips back and forth between Canada and the Maryland eastern shore. She lived in St. Catherines, a Canadian port at the west end of Lake Ontario where many runaways first landed, for some time before eventually settling in Auburn about thirty miles south of Lake Ontario. Frederick Douglass, the well-known black abolitionist speaker and writer who worked and lived in Rochester for many years, knew her well and once wrote in praise of her work, "You, on the other hand, have labored in a private way. I have wrought in the day—you in the night…The midnight sky and the silent stars have been the witnesses of your devotion to freedom and of your heroism. Excepting John Brown—of sacred memory—I know of no one who has willingly encountered more perils and hardships to serve our enslaved people than you have."

Her Auburn house today is a museum with displays on her life and work. Besides being a guide on the Underground Railroad, Tubman later served as an army scout, a spy and a nurse during the Civil War and was eventually awarded a tiny pension for her service to the Union. As a black woman in a time when all women's rights and freedoms were so limited, her exploits, courage, physical stamina and selflessness are little short of incredible. After the Civil War, she worked with Susan B. Anthony and others on the U.S. women's suffrage movement. Sources say she was buried with military honors in the cemetery in Auburn. Sara Hopkins Bradford wrote an interesting account of Tubman's life in *Harriet Tubman: The Moses of Her People*. It was written, in part, to help raise money to support Tubman's efforts to shelter and support poor blacks in Auburn. The entire book is posted online at the University of North Carolina's archive of American Slave Narratives.

Harriet Tubman is probably the best known of the black conductors, but other free blacks, some of them sailors and canal boatmen, also helped runaways get to Canada. In the 1840s, central New York's "burned-over district" made the region fertile ground for abolitionists. Some of the most active white conductors on the railroad were of the Quaker faith.

Many runaways settled in St. Catharines, Ontario, then as now an important shipbuilding center and port on Lake Ontario. St. Catharines was the terminal for the east end of the Welland Canal, and a considerable concentration of marine service businesses built up there, providing work

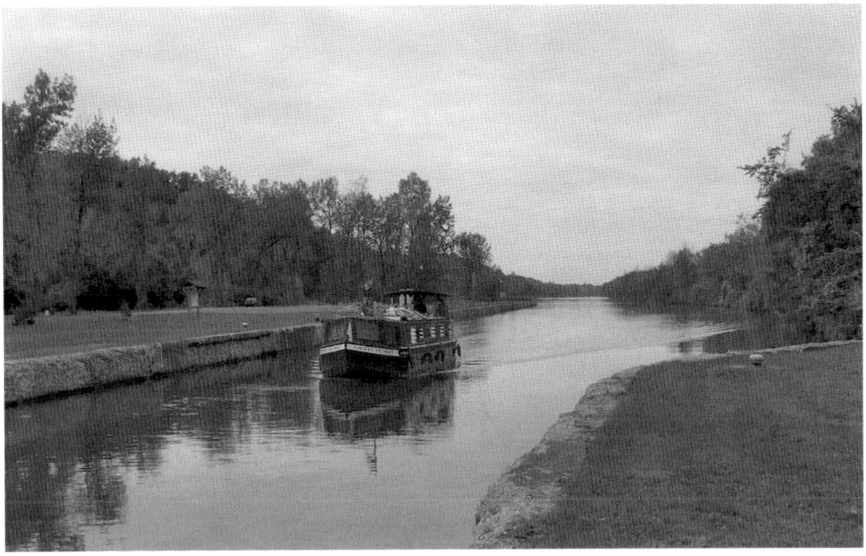

Some runaways were transported via the Erie Canal, shown here in its contemporary form. *Author's collection.*

for some of the escaped slaves. Others went on to inland locations. Some became successful Canadian citizens. Some eventually returned to the United States. Life in Canada was not particularly easy for many of the runaways. Sometimes newly arrived free blacks were swindled and taken advantage of by unscrupulous neighbors. And few of them from the South enjoyed Canadian winters. An interesting account of an escaped slave's experiences in New York and in Canada is the book *Twenty-two Years a Slave, Forty Years a Freeman* by Austin Steward (1793–1860). This text has also been placed online by the University of North Carolina American Slave Narratives.

Steward lived briefly on the shore of Sodus Bay, where his white owner tried to carve a southern plantation-style farm from the forest. He escaped around 1813 but lived in New York State for some time before going to Canada around 1830, where he stayed about six years before coming back to Rochester. Pultneyville's small port was home to several abolitionists, and there is solid written evidence to support the story that Captain Horato Nelson Throop and his neighbor Samuel Cuyler were active "conductors" on the Underground Railroad. Cuyler would hold the runaways until Throop's ship called on its way west along the lakeshore. When the *Ontario* tied up, Cuyler would wander down casually and tell the captain, "I have

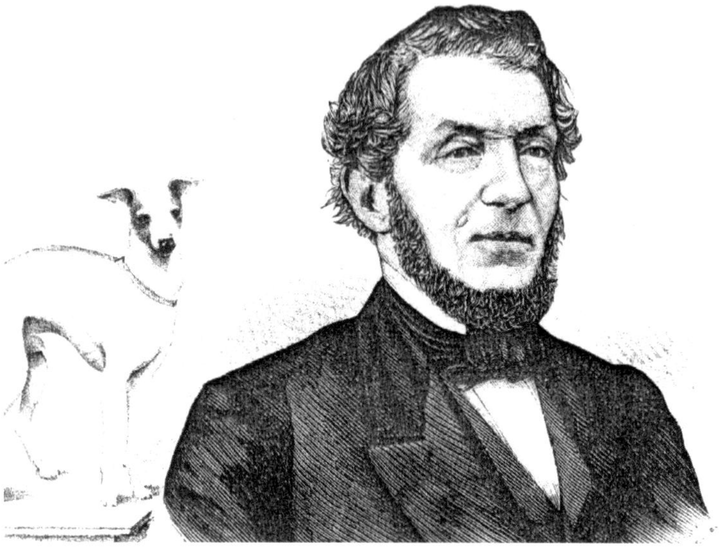

Captain Horatio Nelson Throop smuggled many slaves to Rochester, where they were transferred to Canadian-bound ships. *From W.H. McIntosh's* History of Wayne County.

some passengers for you." Throop was said to then have replied, "My boat runs for passengers" if he believed the coast was clear. Cuyler would wait until after dark to avoid the inevitable bounty hunters who hung around all the ports and then would sneak the slaves through the long piles of cordwood used to fire the ship's boilers.

During Captain Throop's time on the lake, many blacks worked aboard ships in various tasks, and history suggests that more than one black sailor or steamer crew might have quietly served as conductors. We shall probably never know of the countless acts of heroism and altruism by both black and white people that were performed in the face of an evil institution that prevails to this day in various places around the world. They believed in a cause, and they acted, defying what they considered to be an unjust law even as No More Deaths volunteers work today to save the lives of Mexican immigrants lost in the desert along the U.S.-Mexico border. (Their motto is humanitarian aid is never a crime.)

Today, illegal transport of humans continues on and near the lakeshore and in the St. Lawrence River area. The 2008 movie *Frozen River* depicted the movement of illegal immigrants from Canada to the United States via the Akwesasne Mohawk reservation in a realistic and dramatic setting that has the protagonists driving a car loaded with human cargoes across the ice. And several recent articles and stories from the Canadian press cited the transport of Roma (Gypsy) people and other eastern Europeans seeking asylum from the United States to Canada. A recent CBC news story suggests that perhaps 10 percent of Canada's illegal immigrants are being smuggled in by well-organized crime rings that may charge up to $10,000 per person. They come by truck, by shipping container and sometimes aboard yachts and fishing boats. In truth, no one knows how many people are getting over the border headed north or south, though we do know it's been going on for a while. I interviewed a long-retired bootlegger about twenty years ago who recalled that his partner in crime wanted to go into smuggling "Chinamen" into the United States after Prohibition was lifted. And another old neighbor recalled stories of a couple hardy Canadians who hiked across the ice in search of work in rural Wayne County during the Depression-era winter of 1933–34 when the lake froze over. Interestingly, while in the past most of the immigration seemed to be south bound, there are hints that the flow from the United States to Canada may now be increasing, and perhaps because of this, in recent years, the conservative government there has been clamping down on Canada's previously generous policies toward immigrants.

Today, the United States is spending millions of dollars on technology and on thousands of jobs for border patrol officers along the nation's Mexican and Canadian borders. On the northern frontier, drones are flying overhead, cameras and radar monitor key waterways and patrols along the lakeshore and on the water seek to prevent illegal entry. What's been called the world's longest undefended border between two nations is becoming increasingly militarized and turned into what one leftist publication calls a "constitution free zone," where searches and handcuffs can be applied to anyone with no apparent cause. Yet people almost certainly are still slipping across that imaginary line on the map in quests for better lives.

CHAPTER 6

THE SHIP SAVERS

Brave Men and Lucky Vessels

Stories of heroism and courage associated with shipwrecks and rescues of mariners in peril are often told. Less often does one hear of the bold and hardy men who attempted to save ships and cargoes through the process of salvage during Lake Ontario's days of sail and steam. In the nineteenth and early twentieth centuries, the hardy seamen who pulled ships off the rocks or who worked to recover the cargoes of hopelessly damaged vessels were called wreckers. (The term is also used to describe gangs of unscrupulous pirates who would show false signals to lure a ship onto a dangerous shore so that they could murder the crew and steal the cargo and ship's gear and resell it.) Wrecking or salvage, to use the more recent term, on Lake Ontario involved attempts to recover a ship or her cargo after she had been abandoned by her crew. Typically, the salvage crew would negotiate with the insurance underwriters to recover the ship for a set price. If they failed to do so, they would receive no compensation.

Obviously, to be successful at this high-stakes game, those who would salvage a ship had to be extremely good at their trade. They had to know the value of kedges, deadweights, winches, carefully placed cables and old-fashioned leverage for applying large forces. Back then, they didn't have the brute horsepower that today's salvage outfits can employ. Often they had a very limited time to work before the next storm would batter the wreck to pieces. And frequently, they found themselves in dangerous, rapidly changing situations as they worked to move massive objects that sometimes shifted in sudden, unlikely ways. Nonetheless, the lure of quick profits plus the challenge of cheating the lake of its victims drew adventurous men into the field.

Captain Van Cleve in his *Reminiscences* mentions incidents as early as the 1830s of side-wheel steamers towing stranded schooners off the beach. The paddle-wheel steamer was well suited to the task, for she drew little water and could maneuver close to shore. Sometimes the wreckers had to patch a badly holed ship and pump the water out before hauling her off. They often had to remove cargoes in order to do so or to lighten a stranded vessel, shifting the goods to a lighter (barge). This frequently had to be done quickly under less than ideal conditions. (Hardly anybody seems to need salvage on a nice calm summer day.) Sometimes, if a ship was too badly holed to be patched or if she lay in deep water, pontoons were chained or cabled to her and then pumped out or emptied with compressed air similar to submarine buoyancy tanks. When they floated, the ship came up off the bottom, too. She would then be moved inshore until she touched bottom, the pontoons sunk to slack the cables and the process repeated. (Today, salvage operations may use heavy-duty lift bags that are inflated with air during shallow-water operations.) Ships that had rolled over on their sides or capsized could sometimes be righted by heavy lifting derricks or by some tricky maneuvering with tug winch and cable. It all sounds simple, but the devil is in the details. A lot of improvisation often had to happen for jobs to succeed. And there were always unexpected complications from weather, lawyers and other sources. The really successful salvagers had an intuitive feel for the complexities of each job and an ability to make rapid good decisions.

By the Civil War, salvage techniques and equipment were becoming increasingly sophisticated, and steam pumps were increasingly powerful and portable, though the recovery of the schooner *Jamaica* in 1872 was far from routine. It was the subject of several news stories, and the effort succeeded in part because of the midsummer timing of the incident and the quick action taken by her owner.

The *Jamaica*, an Oswego-built ship launched by the Goble shipyard in 1867, was a regular in the grain trade. An account of her launch described her as a canal schooner, sized for the Welland with an eleven-foot hold and a 318-ton measure. On the fateful day, she was loaded with eighteen thousand bushels of wheat and bound from Milwaukee to Oswego. On June 20, while sailing across the south end of Lake Huron, the *Jamaica* was hit by a summer squall and capsized. She went down in seven fathoms (a little over forty feet) of water and took took her unlucky female cook with her. The squall struck about 1:00 p.m., and the hapless Mrs. Weatherhead was below still cleaning up from the noon meal. The wind struck so fast and hard that within minutes the ship was on her beam-ends and water had flooded down into the cabin. The mate, still below eating his dinner, managed to escape through a windward cabin window, but, said the newspaper, the cook was last seen in the kitchen in water nearly up to her armpits. (Her body was later recovered from the cabin when the ship was raised.)

The *Jamaica* was only five years old, and she and her cargo had a combined insured value of $46,000. She lay in shallow water with her masts sticking up above the surface, and her owner, M.M. Wheeler of Oswego, decided to attempt to raise his ship. A week later, he was on the scene with the Coast Wrecking Company's steamer *Rescue* and two pontoons. These large wooden boxes were, according to the news account, 120 feet long, 12 feet deep and 16 feet wide and had boxed-in "wells," much like daggerboard trunks, through which lifting chains or cables could be passed. The summer weather was on Wheeler's side, as calms prevailed, and the wreckers were soon able to pass chains under the ship and up through the pontoon wells to be tightened by jacks. Then the pontoons were flooded and sunk so that they were nearly awash. The chain slings were tightened again and the water pumped out, lifting the pontoons and ship perhaps 10 feet or so off the bottom. The submerged vessel and pontoons were slowly towed toward shore until the schooner grounded. Then the process was repeated. "It was a work of patience," the news reporter wrote, but "entirely successful." The ship merely suffered some damage to her decks, which had "lifted" after the wheat cargo swelled. Thanks to the rapid salvage and the cold water at 40 feet, the ship's cargo hadn't even rotted, and Mr. Wheeler managed to sell his soggy grain to a distillery for a substantial percentage of its insured value.

The newspaper noted his underwriters were so impressed with this shipowner's diligence that they "solicited a photograph of the captain, which it is proposed to have enlarged and suitably framed for an ornament of the general office." The sturdy old *Jamaica* lived on to work for another fifteen years before running ashore with 330 tons of coal in August 1885 on Lake Michigan twenty miles north of Chicago.

The technique used successfully by Mr. Wheeler in 1872 was similar to that employed by Frank Hoffman ninety-seven years later, when he raised the two-masted *Alvin Clark* on Lake Michigan. That ship had also been capsized by a sudden June squall in 1864, a few years before the *Jamaica*. She took her captain and a crew with her and went down in 110 feet of water. Hoffman used a large single barge equipped with winches, and after passing multiple slings under the submerged hull, he and the crew winched her off the bottom and moved inshore into shallower water for another lift. The final lift from shallow water dockside was done with four large cranes on land. The schooner had been sailing light at the time of her sinking, and when Hoffman's volunteer crew finally got her to the surface after two years of work, she was completely intact with virtually no damage. Theodore Karamanski said in his book *Schooner Passage* that even the bilge pumps still worked. The vessel was towed to Menominee and put on exhibit. Unfortunately, when her waterlogged oak timbers and planking dried rapidly and unevenly, they shrank, checked and deteriorated rapidly. In 1994, less than thirty years after her recovery, the *Clark*'s rotting remains were demolished to make way for a parking lot.

The *Clark*'s sorry story probably helped motivate some of the legislation that sought to protect the integrity and artifacts of the many historically significant wooden shipwrecks on the bottom of the Great Lakes. In 1987, a federal law declared these ships to be under the jurisdiction of the state in whose waters they lay. The states promptly followed through, making unauthorized salvage attempts and looting of gear and artifacts illegal. Today's recreational diving community does a superb job of promoting the ethic of "take only photos and leave only bubbles" among underwater tourists.

Another interesting eyewitness account of a nineteenth-century salvage job comes from C.H.J Snider's "Schooner Days" column. It involved individuals who later became known far and wide for their prowess at "wrecking" on Lake Ontario and elsewhere. In 1876, the paddle-wheel steamer *Corinthian* was underway on a September night with about seventy passengers aboard when she struck a rock near Grafton about an hour's steaming east of Cobourg on the lake's north shore. T.M. Kirkwood wrote to Snider:

> *We were going west, and left Kingston at 5 p.m. When we got abreast of Grafton there was a freight train's head light standing still on the tracks ashore, half a mile inland. The first mate, on watch, turned in to the head light, thinking he was at Cobourg. When the train started going west, he discovered the mistake and stopped the* Corinthian*'s headway, but it was too late. We grounded, but we backed her off and we got away for several hundred yards when the steampipe burst, and we drifted ashore again for an all-night bad time. The high sea from the south would lift her and drive her ashore, so much so that in the morning we could walk ashore in three feet of water. In due time Captain Howard who was the manager of the Richelieu and Ontario Navigation Company sent two powerful steamers, the* Hiram A. Calvin *and the* Chieftain, *with steam pumps in charge*

> *of Captain Donnelly and his son from Garden Island. They pumped her dry, and lightened her more by dismantling the paddle wheels, draining the boilers, and putting the freight and furniture ashore. They made a rope fast to a stick of cordwood through a port hole in the forecastle.* [Then] *both steamers backed up as close as possible and made a run.*
>
> *This tore a hole in her iron hull without moving her. Next they made the rope fast to a long elm fender* [log] *inside of the hull, and both vessels kept jerking her off, little by little. When* [they got her] *afloat they took her to Cobourg, and a diver went under her and found a large boulder fastened to her bottom, which could not be removed. Captain Howard gave orders to tow us to Montreal with a tow boat on each side of the* Corinthian, *but, as a storm blew up again the tow boats made matchwood of our* [paddle wheel] *guards and he made them let go and tow ahead. All hands were aboard of the tow boats with the exception of Captain Howard, Captain Donnelly and his son, and myself. At that time I was in my teens and made up my mind that I would rather stay on the* Corinthian *than aboard of the tow boats. As she was lightened* [with no cargo aboard] *she got tossed like a cork until we reached Kingston. May I say that I crossed the Atlantic forty-four times and did not get tossed as bad as going down the lake on the* Corinthian *that night. Perhaps I am the only man alive to-day, with the exception of Captain Donnelly's son, that was aboard of the* Corinthian *going down the lake on that stormy night.*

The Donnelly Brothers was one of the lake's best-known and most successful salvage firms of the day.

Donnelly's, based in Kingston, was founded in 1890, according to incorporation papers posted online "for the acquisition and leasing of wrecking plant and the employment thereof for the saving of vessels and for all purposes connected with wrecking." Before that, Great Lakes historian Walter Lewis wrote, John Donnelly Sr. worked for the Calvins of Garden Island in their salvage program.

The firm's name appears in a 1905 news story on the attempt to raise a steamer lost off the Thousand Islands Park in 105 feet of water. At the time, two brothers, Thomas and John, were running the business, their father having died shortly before. Apparently the ship eluded them, for the story notes that its remains were disturbed during Seaway construction fifty years later and slipped into even deeper water. But the Donnellys saved many other vessels through their skill and hard work. They made money at it, too.

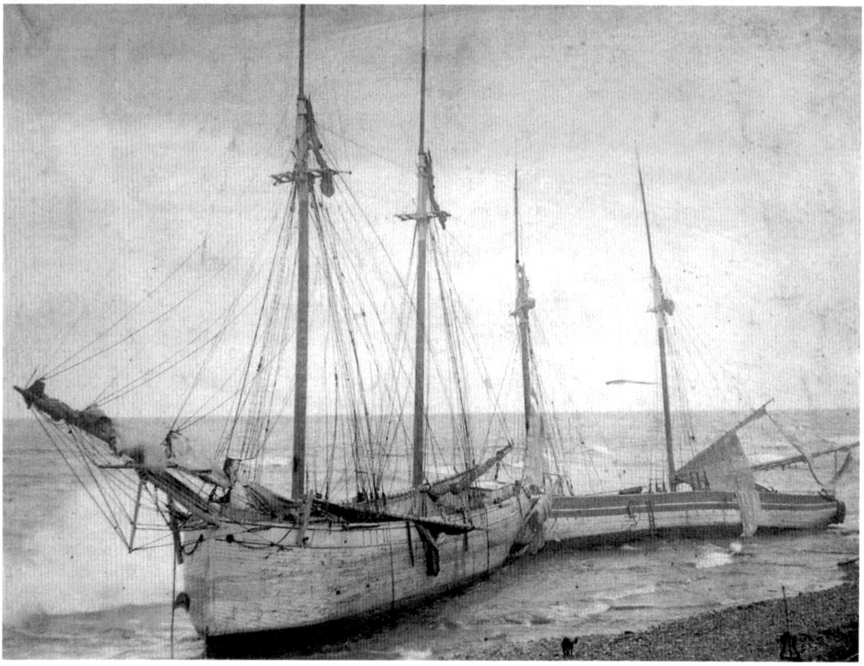

The wreckers got the *D.G. Fort* (foreground) off after she grounded on Pelee Island, but she went to pieces here at Oswego in November 1894. *Photo from Walter Lewis.*

A 1910 shipping directory lists a half dozen salvage, or wrecking, companies on the lake, including the Calvin Company and Donnelly's. The directory equipment listing for the Calvins gives an idea of the technology of the time. It included two tugs, the *Johnston* and *Frontenac*, with derricks for handling pumps and equipped with powerful steam winches and "wires" for releasing vessels stranded in swift water. The firm also owned the "light draft" side-wheel steamers *Chieftain* and *Parthia* with steam hoists. The company listing included "ten centrifugal and twelve inch rotary pumps wires, chains, diving gear etc." The Calvins were mainly a timber-forwarding operation. They made huge log rafts and sent them down to Montreal using the current of the St. Lawrence. Salvage was a sideline business for them.

The Donnellys at that time had the side-wheel steamer *Donnelly* and the screw steamer *Lloyd's* with "lighterage capacity" of 300 tons. They also had two lighters of 750 tons with steam winches and other facilities to handle cargo quickly. The directory also listed eight steam pumps (including a "cataract coal pump") and necessary screw jacks and chains for deep-water work. Their modified paddle-wheel steamer *Cornwall* only drew about six feet in her wrecking configuration.

The early twentieth century was probably close to the peak for the salvage business on Lake Ontario. By the 1920s, business began to drop off as the old wooden ships and sailing schooners were laid up and replaced by bigger steel-hulled vessels with more powerful engines. The demise of the tug and consort business also contributed to less wrecking. The postwar recession on the lakes was the final nail in the coffin, and by the 1920s, the Donnellys often didn't get more than one job a year. They were bought out around 1928, but the brothers were kept on to run the salvage business for a few years longer. It was their skill rather than the equipment inventory that really made the business work.

When the Great Depression arrived, shippers and insurance companies increasingly abandoned ships rather than spend money on their salvage. It was quicker and cheaper to simply blow the hulks up.

But before that, Donnelly Brothers salvaged dozens of vessels, many of which went back to work earning profits for their owners. Walter Lewis told of one, the little steamer *Rosedale* that ran aground on Charity Shoal in 1897 and was abandoned as a total loss. The underwriters hired the Donnellys to get her off, and the steamer went on to work for many more years

The steel-hulled *Rosedale* was launched in England in 1888 and was sized to fit the locks of the St. Lawrence. She was only 174 feet long and displaced 1,040 gross tons. She was built to carry either bulk cargoes or higher-value package freight. The steamer often carried grain and was navigated from an open bridge atop a small amidships deck house and was flush decked with two masts used both for auxiliary sail and for cargo handling. In 1890, she was lengthened to 246 feet and given a third mast. In 1892, her insured value was $115,000.

Charity Shoal (named for the unfortunate schooner that "discovered" it to her terminal regret in the early 1800s) lies right in the pathway of shipping bound up or down the lake from the St. Lawrence River. This rocky shoal lies in an area where magnetic disturbances often plagued old-time sailors when visibility was bad. The *Rosedale* piled up on it on December 4 and was declared a total loss, but the Donnellys got her off. For $17,000, they patched her up, pumped her out and towed her stern first into port for repairs. It took them just a week.

Not all the salvage jobs were done by professionals with specialized equipment. An interesting DIY recovery of an old-timer that went ashore a couple miles east of Rochester was written up in the Rochester newspaper

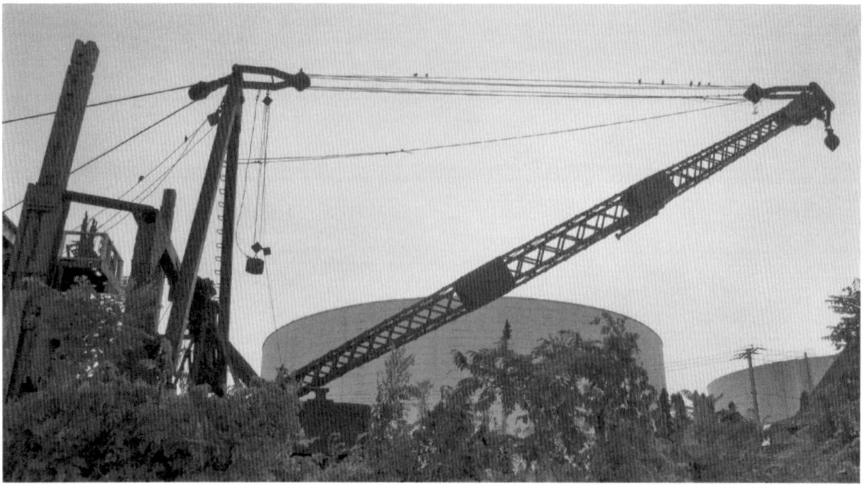

The steam-powered derrick barge displayed at Oswego's H.L. White Museum (its crane is shown here) was salvaged by volunteers from the bottom of the New York Canal System. *Author's collection.*

in 1894. The tough old canal-sized schooner *Singapore* had seen seventeen years of service when she was blown onto the beach during a bad squall in August. She must have been sailing light without a cargo, because after she went ashore her crew stripped her gear, jacked her up and blocked the vessel out of reach of the winter waves and left. (Recall, the old canalers were essentially flat bottomed and had centerboards so they didn't need a lot of water to float when their holds were empty.) During the winter, she was sold to a Captain Malcomson of Hamilton, who replaced one plank and did some caulking on her bottom and otherwise got her back in shape to float. The following spring—using lots of ingenuity, low-tech engineering, simple gear and the ship's own anchors and capstan to prepare the ways—the crew launched her off the beach.

"The preparations for launching the boat were made with patience and care," reported the newspaper. Four ways made up of wooden beams were arranged for the boat to slide sideways into the water. Each way was made with three pieces of timber mortised and fastened together to make a piece 115 feet long, extending from the boat into the water. The heavy timbers of the ways were fastened to the shore by a chain attached to a "deadman" anchor made from a tree trunk buried in an oblong, three-foot-deep excavation in the ground on the shore, transverse to the direction of the ways. The timbers of each of the ways were placed parallel to each other and fastened together.

They also had to be blocked up and supported in the water, and this was one of the last things the crew did before attempting the launch of the hundred-plus-ton schooner. (Any rough water would obviously be a problem for keeping piles of rocks or cribbing under the timbers in place.)

The fastening together of the lengths of heavy timbers that formed the ways when laid end to end "was done easily," said the news story. A derrick (a heavy pole) was fastened to the ship's anchor, which was then carried out and dropped a couple hundred feet offshore. A line was led through a block on the end of the anchored derrick pole to the second long timber. The other end connected to a cable that was then wound around the ship's capstan, drawing the timber out to the desired position where it was mortised to the first section on land. The third timber was then pulled out in the same manner and mortised to the second timber, making a continuous way 115 feet long. The crew made four ways of heavy timbers. When all was in place and the ways had been greased for the launch, a call went in to Charlotte for a tug to pull the *Singapore* off the beach and down the ways.

She made it off, for the *History of Hamilton Harbor* by Ivan S. Brookes records that she was back to work carrying coal for her new owner that summer. But ten years later, the old ship's luck ran out. The *Buffalo Evening News* of September 16, 1904, records the *Singapore* once again went ashore, this time on Lake Huron near the entrance of Kincardine Harbor. She was loaded with lumber and "was dashed to pieces." The owner, his wife, three children and the ship's crew of five all were rescued.

Thanks to satellite GPS, radar, reliable diesels and other technology, maritime disasters on the lake are far less common than a century ago. But accidents still happen. In 2012, a big tug underway off Prince Edward County suffered an engine fire that killed one crew member and caused extensive damage to the ship. The most recent big wreck I know of at Oswego happened in 1964 and resulted in a tale told to me by one of the people involved in its salvage, Ed Moriarity of Fair Haven. It was a salvage effort that involved brave (or foolish) young men and a tanker full of gasoline on Oswego's doorstep.

The events took place shortly after Moriarity had graduated from college with no job prospects. A 230-foot tanker barge, the *Val 51* (formerly the motorship *Lio*), pushed by the tug *Joan Kehoe*, left Oswego for a tank farm in Ogdensburg on the St. Lawrence on the evening of June 16, but the barge broke loose in a storm shortly after leaving port. The barge drifted ashore down near St. Paul's Cemetery. She was loaded with gasoline, hundreds of thousands of gallons of it.

A cold front had just swept through, bringing stiff winds and building seas. As the tug and barge worked offshore, the night wind grew stronger, and the waves built rapidly. After about two hours, the tug captain decided it would be prudent to turn back to Oswego. At 1:00 a.m., the captain decided to take the two-man crew of the barge off. They anchored in about four hundred feet of water, got the men safely aboard the tug and returned to Oswego aboard the *Kehoe*. But the barge, anchored on poor holding and rock, soon went adrift. It quickly blew ashore in the building waves and thirty-plus-knot north winds. It soon "crunched to a halt on the rocky bottom in nine to ten feet of water about three hundred feet off the Hammermill Plant," according to the local newspaper.

"Crunched" might not be quite the best verb to describe the impact. When 2,366 tons of highly explosive gasoline plus steel barge, machinery and other gear hits the rocks with a near gale behind it, maybe slam, screech, crash or kaboom might be more accurate. At any rate, according to the story, at least one compartment tore open, and an unknown quantity of gasoline spilled into the seething breakers. Pretty shortly thereafter, the newspaper said, the phones at the Oswego police station started ringing. People were complaining about a strong odor of gasoline. Had a service station fuel tank burst open? Or did a pipeline somewhere nearby fail? Police, Coast Guardsmen, the Oswego fire chief, Hammermill electricians and workers and other interested bystanders gathered at the scene to determine if an evacuation was needed. Luckily for Oswego, if not for the *Val 51*, that night, the wind was blowing thirty-four miles per hour according to the Oswego Lighthouse watch. That presumably dissipated the fumes and kept the Hammermill Plant and adjacent properties from going up in a massive fireball.

The big tug *Anna Moran* was sent for, and after the wind and waves dropped off, she left Ogdensburg and hurried to the scene. The tug had the needed horsepower to get the *Val 51* and her remaining cargo of liquid dynamite off the rocks and into Oswego Harbor. There the wreck was grounded on the sandbar that lies right where the riprap breakwater ends and the cement pier begins. A crew then began the three-week salvage job.

Ed recalled that a friend, the nephew of Sequin Salvage's CEO, called him up and said, "Put on the oldest, most ragged clothes you got. And don't ask any questions." Off he went, along with a couple dozen other men. They didn't allow any married workers. It was too dangerous, he said. He remembered they were out there for about fifty hours straight. The salvage boss had scoured four counties to find brass tools to reduce the chances of striking a spark: "If that gas went off, it would have been the biggest

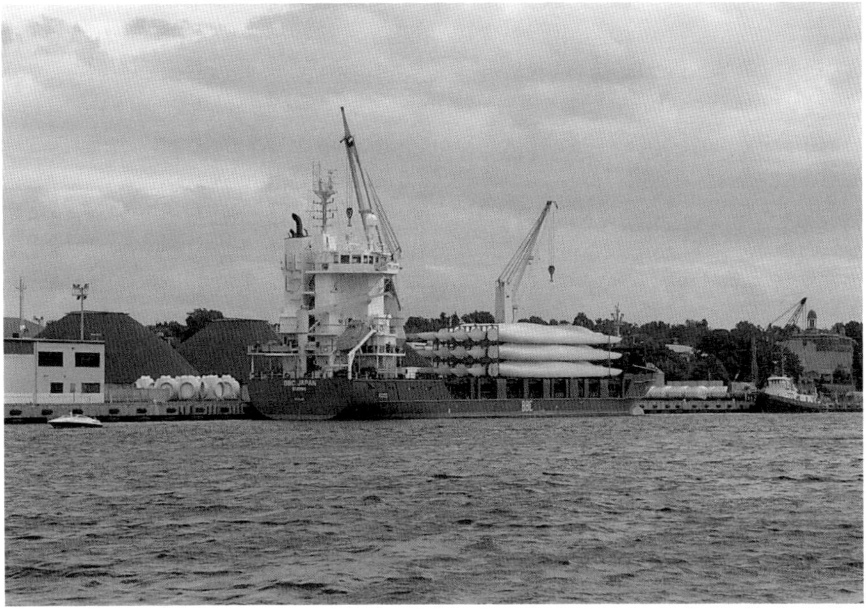

Oswego Harbor today is still a commercial port. *Author's collection.*

explosion Oswego had ever seen." (It could well have been something on the order of the munitions ship that exploded in Halifax Harbor back in 1917, killing two thousand people and leveling five hundred acres of the city in what is today considered the largest man-made explosion predating the atom bomb.)

One of the first things they had to do was get rid of the rest of the cargo. The barge had been holed and some or all of the cargo tanks filled. The gasoline, originally 700,000 gallons of it, naturally floated to the top and kept the barge from sinking. But before they could seal the holes and pump out the water, they had to deal with the gas. This they did. They did it in the dark of night with an eight-inch pump. The next morning, 99 percent of the gas was gone. No one asked questions. The newspaper account of the wreck's initial grounding stated that an "unknown quantity of gasoline entered the lake." And as Ed remarked in his telling of the tale, "It happened a long time ago."

Regretfully, the next morning there were still a few gallons sloshing around on top of the water in each flooded compartment, more than enough to generate a potentially deadly explosion as they emitted a dangerous mix of oxygen and gas fumes. One Internet site states that a single gallon of gas in vapor form is equivalent to about eighty-three pounds of dynamite. One suspects that the conditions inside the reeking compartments filled with fumes after they sealed the holes and pumped air in to blow out the water must have been pretty unimaginable. Ed did recall that a couple of the hardhat divers got gasoline inside their suits and had to go ashore. "We were always thinking about where the wind was as we worked so we would know which way to jump," he explained. The divers jammed wedges and scraps of wood into the tears and holes in the barge bottom plates and then used air compressors and pumps to dry out the compartments.

Ed remembered the big trash pumps kept plugging up. There had been a couple fifty-gallon barrels full of towels in the barge's machinery room. The towels kept getting sucked into the pumps. You could tell by the sound when a pump plugged. The crew would quickly shut it down to remove the towels. They were motivated to move fast because when the pumps clogged, sparks would come out of the muffler. (There was still plenty of gasoline floating around on top of the water at this point.)

Eventually, they got most of the water out and were then able to put hard patches on the holes so that the barge could travel to a drydock for repairs. To seal the biggest holes in the bottom of the barge, Ed remembered, they used an ungodly mix of mattresses, cyclone chain-link fencing, poured-in-place concrete and channel steel. They got the mattresses from an old hotel in Oswego and plugged the holes. You'd think it would be easy to sink a mattress, but Ed assured me that it's not. They don't waterlog nearly as fast as you would imagine. But eventually, the crew got them hauled and pushed and tugged and tussled into place and secured with a wad of fencing pressed tight between the channel iron on the outside and what remained of the barge bottom on the inside. They welded a long threaded rod to the channel iron. The rod protruded through the patch to the inside of the boat. There, a big nut was tightened down on it to compress the patch tight before they poured concrete into the bottom of the compartment to further seal everything. There was considerable trial and error in the process, so it wasn't nearly as easy as it sounds.

It took several weeks to get the barge stabilized enough to be transported to a drydock down on Staten Island via the barge canal. Ed recalled that he and his friend Robbie got temporary memberships in the freshwater maritime union for the trip. They went as deck hands, and for the most part, the trip was uneventful as the patch job held up just fine. One night, however, proved an exception. The tug captain needed to make a fuel stop. It was on the Hudson River, and there was a current running as there usually is in rivers. The tug driver seriously miscalculated the strength of the current, and Ed and his friend, who had been sitting up on the front of the barge enjoying the nice summer stars overhead, suddenly saw themselves heading straight for a mass of huge timbers looming out of the darkness with heaven only knows how many hundreds of tons of momentum behind them. They leapt for their lives and scrambled to safety as huge timbers splintered and snapped and flew like twigs in the air.

Happily, a few days later they made it safely to the shipyard and its drydock. When the barge had been blocked up and pumped out, Ed recalled walking around under it and marveling at the number of holes in its bottom. Some of them were perfectly round where a boulder had poked up into the vessel. The whole effort to save the tanker had been futile. She was too severely damaged to be worth repair. But the salvage crew got its money.

Alas, not too long after that, the Sequin Salvage Company itself ran terminally aground on the shoals of shaky finances. As Ed recalled, its principal manager, an ex-combat engineer, was a genius at rigging and salvage jobs. But he wasn't a suit and tie man. He liked to go to auctions and buy stuff that would be surely useful someday, somewhere in the business. He had big plans and ideas, but, Ed said, he sort of lost focus. And money. After he ran out of money, that was the end of Sequin Salvage.

You don't hear so much about salvage now. Often a ship or yacht is destroyed where it lies or is hauled off for scrapping. One hundred years ago, ships were still worth salvaging. Maybe they were better built then or capital cost more. These days, all too often, when a yacht goes ashore and suffers minor damage, the insurance company totals it, the owner walks and the boat goes to a landfill. It's all in keeping with our disposable society. But folk musician Stan Roger's "The *Mary Ellen Carter*," an inspirational tune about triumph over great odds as the crew salvages their old ship remains one of his most popular songs ever.

CHAPTER 7

LEGENDARY YACHTS OF LAKE ONTARIO

Recreational boating has been part of upstate New York's history and culture for nearly two hundred years. Our diverse and varied waterways include tiny wilderness lakes, large rivers, placid canals and two Great Lakes. Our waters have nurtured an array of distinctive boat designs and types of national renown.

Within a generation of the first settlement of these well-watered shores, a few men had acquired enough wealth and leisure to indulge in boating for fun. In those times of sparse populations and no all-weather roads, water was a vital mode of transportation. Many pioneer homesteaders in the lakeshore region were New Englanders, recently removed from the coast. Salt water still ran in their veins, and seafaring skills were widespread among them. Some promptly put their skills to use on the lake.

C.H.J. Snider wrote that yachts were sailing Lake Ontario by the mid-1830s. The first organized boating club on Lake Ontario was established in Toronto around 1850, just a few years after the venerable New York Yacht Club's founding. Fishing and hunting camps and summer homes were being built in the Thousand Islands area of the St. Lawrence even before railroads had made it an easy overnight trip from New York City to Watertown or Alexandria Bay. Seth Green of Rochester, a pioneer in fish hatchery techniques, is said to have purchased the first St. Lawrence vacation spot. He paid forty dollars for an island in 1854 with the intent of "studying" the river's fish on summer evenings (with fishing pole in hand, we assume).

After the Civil War and the rapid rise of industrialization and associated growing middle class of artisans, clerks and craftsmen, pleasure boating became a widespread diversion. Though the men (and boating was then overwhelmingly a male-dominated sport) were bankers, scribes or store keepers, living memory of the working mariners' arts was still widespread among yacht owners whose fathers or grandfathers had sailed blue water as mates or bosuns. By the 1870s, boat shops along the Finger Lakes, Lake Ontario and on the St. Lawrence were turning out thousands of canoes, rowboats and small sailing craft, most of them built of readily available oak, pine, elm and northern white cedar from local forests. Shipyards on Lake Ontario and the St. Lawrence built steam yachts and big sloops and schooners as splendid as any to be found on salt water between 1870 and 1930.

The natural resources, money and human energy of upstate New York gave rise to an era of craftsmanship and innovation in pleasure boat design that quickly became widely known and respected. Today, some of those New York–built boats from our inland waters remain preserved in museums and boathouses of wealthy collectors. The Antique Boat Museum in Clayton calls itself North America's premier freshwater nautical museum and houses hundreds of pleasure boats, nearly all of which were built by upstate craftsmen or brought to the St. Lawrence by wealthy summer residents. The museum also hosts one of the longest-running antique boat shows in the country.

The St. Lawrence River was a hot bed of early power boating activity, with speed records and race boat design innovations of national significance. However, that history has been well documented, and I will gloss over those glorious (and noisy) mahogany hulled Gold Cup boats and zippy home built hydroplanes so popular on protected bays and on stretches of the St. Lawrence to concentrate on quiet boating.

Three nineteenth-century upstate New York boats and boat builders of national reputation were the canoes and rowboats of the J.H. Rushton Company in Canton, the St. Lawrence Skiff and the Adirondack Guide boat. The legendary Adirondack Guide boat, strong and buoyant enough to carry a guide, his sportsman client and a dead deer yet light enough to portage between mountain lakes, is not part of our lakeshore region's history, though upstate boat shops are still building these sleek rowing craft and selling them at five-figure prices to collectors of fine wooden boats. However, the St. Lawrence Skiff from the Thousand Islands and the canoes of the Rushton Company saw wide use on Lake Ontario. The builder of a twenty-three-foot sailboat I once owned recalled sailing around the lake with a St. Lawrence Skiff in the 1920s, and Rushton sailing canoes were among

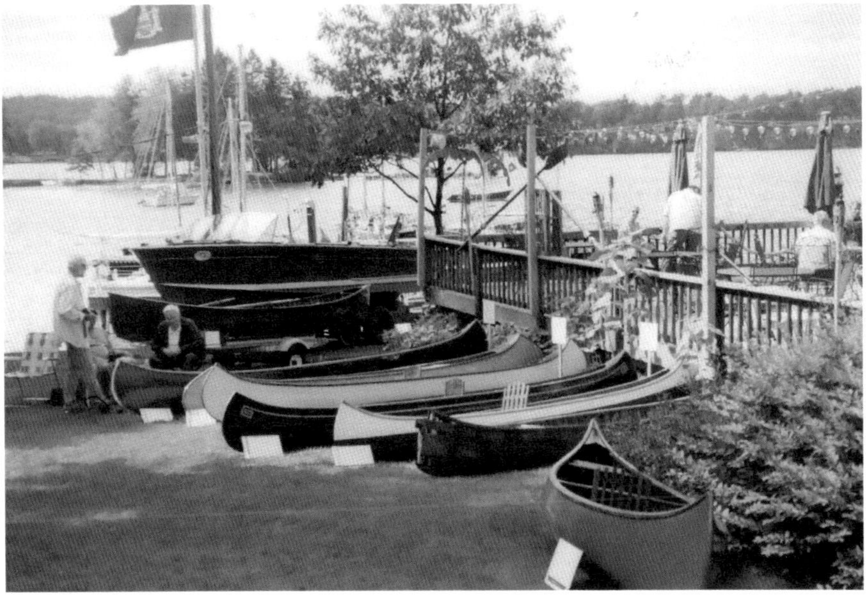

Antique boat shows like this with a lineup of "Canadian" canoes are now popular. *Photo by Greg Grunditsch.*

the racing fleet of the Rochester Canoe Club, founded on Irondequoit Bay in 1882. Rochester was also home to George Ruggles, a sailing canoe builder in the 1880s, whose boats gained an international reputation for their speed. Captain Ruggles is also remembered as the inventor of an effective rotary snowplow used on the electric interurban trolley lines in the early 1900s. He was a respected lake captain, had part ownership of the schooner *H.M. Ballou* and brought the first tug to Charlotte, which he was captain of for several years. He built his first canoe, the *Safronia*, in 1884, and she proved to be a winner.

The sailing canoe evolved into an extreme speedster that demanded great skill from its skipper. These slippery little boats generally had two masts, lots of sail and a sliding plank that the single-handing skipper used to move his weight far out over the water to keep the narrow boat from capsizing. Racing sailing canoes was not a sport for the faint of heart back then.

After the Civil War, two distinctly different types of canoes came into use in our area—the open so-called Canadian canoe for paddling (see boat show photo above), and the decked sailing canoe in a slightly less extreme form than that adopted by the racers. Many hardy young men traveled the

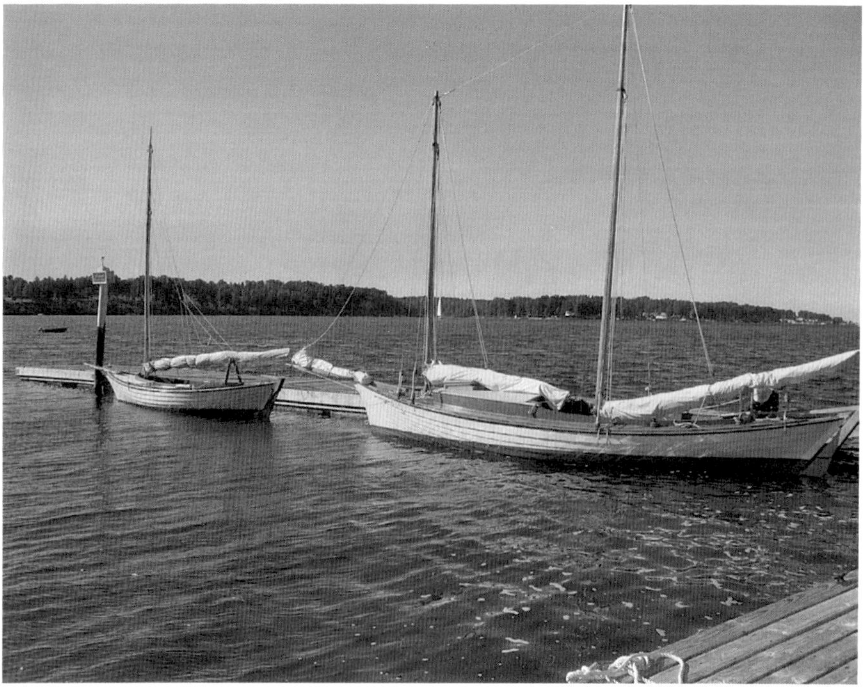

Some 1890s decked sailing canoes were used as camp cruisers, much as these open sailing boats are used today by hardy travelers. *Author's collection.*

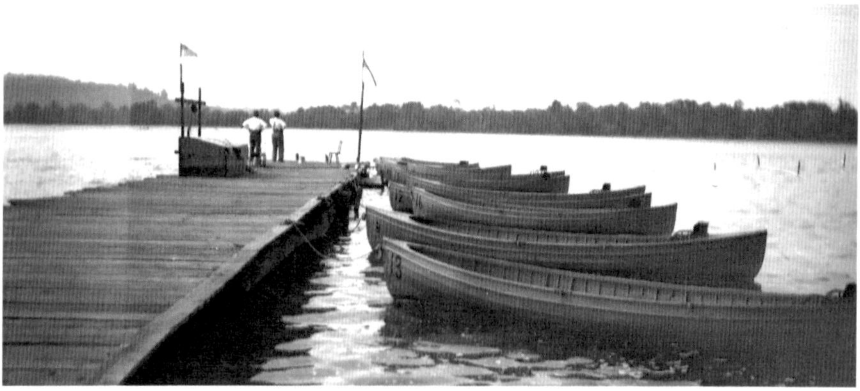

St. Lawrence Skiff rental fleet at the Fair Haven State Park, early 1930s. *Photo by Edna Williams.*

lake and St. Lawrence River with these tiny cruisers after being inspired by the writing of the British canoe cruiser John McGregor, who traveled widely through Europe and the Middle East with his "Rob Roy," a wooden-decked canoe. His book, *A Thousand Miles in the Rob Roy Canoe*, launched the sport in England and here, too. One of the best-known upstate New York canoe cruisers was a shoemaker named George Washington Sears, who wrote about his travels in an early sporting publication called *Forest and Stream* under the pen name of Nessmuk. He ordered a small lightweight boat from the Rushton Company that could be carried from one lake to another in the Adirondacks. Named for a Dickens character, the wooden lapstrake hull of the *Sairy Gamp* weighed just under eleven pounds. It is on exhibit today in the Smithsonian. Sears wrote in 1880 of his craft, "Having the summer before me, designing to haunt the nameless lakes and streams not down on the maps, and not caring to hire a guide, it stands to reason that my canoe should be of the lightest, and she is. Perhaps she is the lightest cedar-built canoe in the United States, or anywhere else." The canoe may well have been just that, and Nessmuk's articles helped publicize the high quality of boats from Canton-based Rushton Company. At its production peak, the business turned out hundreds of canoes, rowboats and small sailboats each year. The Rushton shop exhibited a line of boats at the World Columbian Exhibition in 1893, and today, a Rushton-built rowing boat or canoe in good condition is worth thousands of dollars.

One of the shop's mainstays was the double-ended St. Lawrence Skiff, a heavy but easy rowing boat generally sixteen to twenty-two feet in length. Unlike the lightweight canoes, these boats did not have to be portaged, and their weight and stability were well suited to the sometimes choppy and windy St. Lawrence River. A heavier boat had momentum to push through the one- to two-foot waves while traveling the open stretches of the river. St. Lawrence Skiffs were also sometimes sailed without rudders. The crew steered by shifting its weight around the boat. With its sleek lines and long length, the St. Lawrence Skiff was so easy to row that often a fishing guide would travel twenty miles under oars during the day with his party in search of a trophy muskellunge or a big pike. After President Grant visited the Thousand Islands in 1872 and spent three days fishing from a skiff, the boat type gained national recognition. They were widely built in boat shops throughout the Finger Lakes region and were tremendously popular for both rowing and sailing. Back in 1920, a top-of-the-line, fancy grade skiff with curly maple end decks and a mahogany sheer strake built by the Skaneateles Boat & Canoe Company would go for $235 (when the average working wage was about $1,200 a year). Today, they are still built in fiberglass and wood, and a hundred-year-old antique in good shape could cost you close to $10,000.

Along with a rich diversity of small pleasure boats, the wide waters of Lake Ontario were also home to large, elegant yachts that rivaled the toys and playthings of the wealthy East Coast tycoons in the days before income taxes. The three-masted schooner *Oriole* of Toronto, second of three big yachts of that name, measured 131 feet from boom end to bowsprit tip. Other notable yachts on Lake Ontario and the St. Lawrence included the steam yacht *Clover*, owned by George Boldt—the hotel magnate best known for his huge stone castle on Heart Island—the three-masted *Azara* that spread 6,000 square feet of sail and once sailed twenty-nine miles in just under two hours and the 220-ton Canadian *Countess of Dufferin* that challenged for the America's Cup in 1876. (She was decisively defeated.) George Boldt also owned a "houseboat," *La Duchess*, that was 106 feet long. She was built in 1903 of wood, though after World War II the tired hull was replaced with steel. Her last owner donated her to the Clayton Antique Boat Museum, and the boat is now open to the public. She features a fancy stained-glass skylight, gold-leaf stencils, a brass fireplace and vintage furniture and is a rare glimpse back in time to the leisure lifestyle of the rich a century ago.

With the exception of the Boldt houseboat *La Duchess*, these elegant mega yachts from the gilded age are long gone. But one legendary Lake Ontario yacht, the 126-foot steam yacht *Cangarda*, still lives and sails thanks to an extraordinary restoration effort. She is one of only three Edwardian-era steam yachts still afloat and is the only surviving U.S.-built steamer of this era. She now sails the East Coast, but for most of her life, the steel-hulled yacht roamed fresh water. And from 1954 until 1983, she served as a floating home for a Rochester-area resident named Fred Smith. Charlotte riverfront watchers may recall seeing the yacht's graceful white hull tied up next to the railroad station on the west side of the river just north of the Stutson Street bridge. Smith, a retired architect, was a steam nut who recognized the unique value of the old yacht with its Cuban mahogany woodwork, leaded glass light fixtures, Tiffany skylight and vintage all-original steam engine. He kept the engine oiled, turned it over occasionally and generally looked after the big yacht as best as he could. I visited aboard when I heard the steamer was about to leave the river. Smith had sold her to another, wealthier steamboat fancier, and she was about to be towed down the river to Massachusetts to be hauled out and restored. He also gave me a bit of her history.

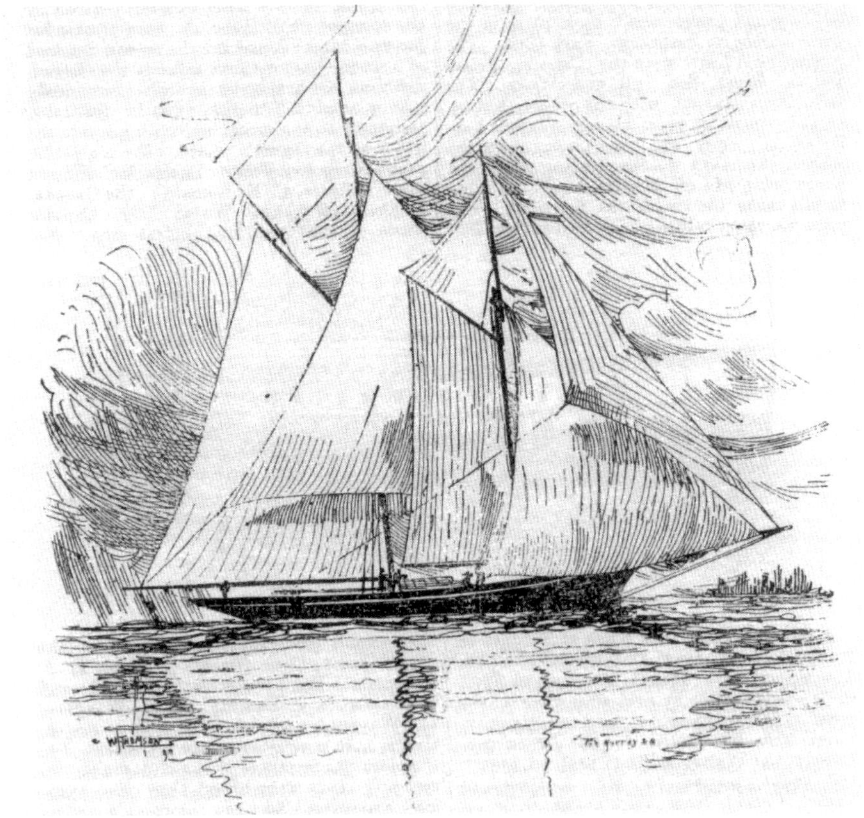

Schooner *Oriole*, Royal Canadian Yacht Club, owned by the Gooderham family whose distillery was one of Canada's biggest whiskey producers. *From* Maritime History of the Great Lakes.

The yacht was built in 1901 at the Pusey and Jones shipyard of Wilmington, Delaware, a yard that launched several other notable and long-lived iron-hulled ships, including *Albatross I*, the first U.S. Fish Commission steamer designed purely for research. *Cangarda*, however, was built of less corrosion-resistant steel for a Michigan lumber baron. She came to Lake Ontario just a couple years later, after being purchased by a wealthy Canadian, George Fulford, who is remembered for being a Canadian senator. The yacht resided for a number of years on the St. Lawrence as *Magedoma*, and when World War II came along, she served as a Canadian training ship on Lake Ontario. Fred Smith bought her after the war in 1954 and lived aboard year-round for nearly thirty years in his cluttered bachelor quarters on the Genesee. Despite being a freshwater

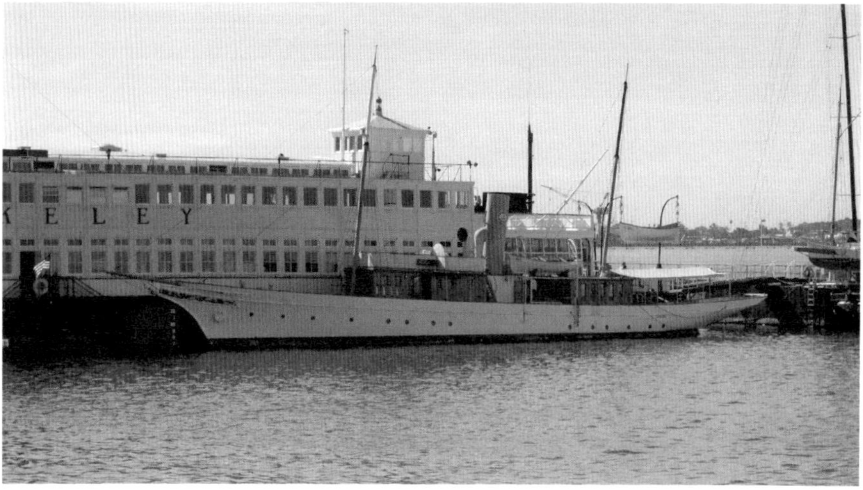

Edwardian-era steam yacht *Medea*, similar in age, size and type to *Cangarda*, at the Maritime Museum of San Diego. *Author's collection.*

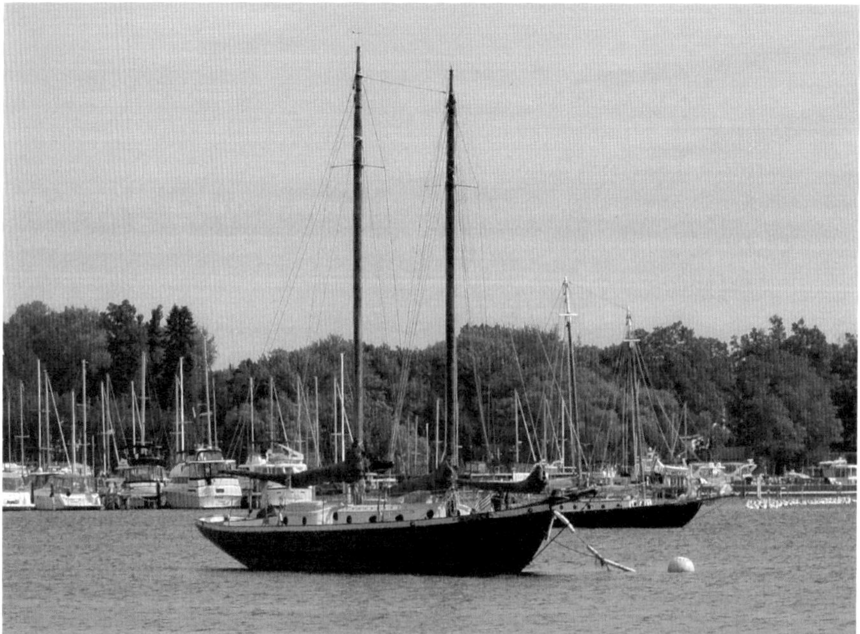

Lotus on her mooring in Sodus Bay, 2012. *Author's collection.*

boat, the steel hull was badly rusted (haul out facilities for maintaining 126 footers being nonexistent in Charlotte). There were a number of perilously thin spots in the riveted plates below the water, and Smith explained that the buyer was going to wrap a giant heavy plastic bag around the hull as insurance for the tow down the canal and up the coast to Gloucester.

Cangarda made it, and a year or so later, I was in New England and stopped off to check on the restoration progress. Richard Reedy, the owner, had by then completely stripped out the hull. All the yacht's interior bits and pieces were labeled and inventoried and filled a sizable portion of a big warehouse. The steam engine had been sent off to be restored and work begun on putting a new bottom in the hull. After that, I heard no more of the *Cangarda* until she popped up on the Internet as being "restored" a few years ago. From the Internet, I learned that after my visit to the Gloucester site, money and time ran out. Several years and $850,000 had been spent when Reedy gave the project up. The stripped-out hull sank in Boston Harbor and was about to be scrapped when it was saved at the last minute. A buyer was found for all the bits and pieces of poor *Cangarda*. Robert McNeil, a venture capitalist in biomedical start-up firms, purchased the remains and had them transported across the country. Restoration ensued in California, and $12 million dollars and six years later, the boat was relaunched with much of its original machinery and virtually all its furnishings intact. One person touring the boat described the effort as "astounding."

In 2011, the *Cangarda*'s new owner had her transported via a ship through the Panama Canal to Florida. She then steamed north to New York and the Hudson and then through the canal and Lake Ontario. She cruised down the St. Lawrence to her old haunts at Brockville, where she had been the pampered yacht of the Fulford family. Here she celebrated a home coming of sorts, lying alongside the residence that had once been the Fulford boathouse. Fred Smith had long since slipped his mooring and made his final passage, but the boat he had devoted himself to keeping afloat for three decades appears set to enjoy another hundred years of service. As a friend of Smith's commented, "I'm sure he's smiling now."

Another old-timer that has been a familiar sight on local waters for over ninety years sails Sodus Bay. The sixty-foot gaff-rigged schooner *Lotus*, launched around 1918 from a boatyard on Rocky River, Ohio, as the *Miss Gloucester*, served the Comstock family for sixteen years. She briefly sailed Lake Erie before coming to Lake Ontario in 1922. The Comstocks of Newark named her after the famous exotic water flowers that once covered the south end of the bay.

Lotus sailed with them until 1938 before getting new owners and a new name. In 1943, she got another longtime owner who kept her going until her donation to the Sea Scouts in 1971. By then, *Lotus* was a fifty-plus-year-old wooden boat in an era of low-maintenance fiberglass craft. The costs of keeping an old wooden boat in good shape using hired help were formidable, and few people were willing or able to spend the time needed to do the job themselves. But the Sea Scouts had, at least in theory, a large number of helping hands to splice and serve, sand, caulk, paint and otherwise keep a big wooden boat fit. For twenty years, a volunteer force of kids and adults labored to keep the seventeen-ton schooner operational. Time, however, has a way of catching up with old steel-fastened wooden hulls. Like many a wooden boat before and since, entropy was getting the upper hand. By the 1990s, *Lotus* needed serious structural work. A former owner kicked in a substantial sum of money for a professional rebuild, and the Scouts matched it with a grant. *Lotus* was trucked to Rhode Island to get a new stem, a new laid pine deck, deck beams and other work.

When *Lotus* first arrived on Sodus Bay, a few commercial sailing vessels were still calling on the port to load coal at the trestle or to deliver cedar posts from Canada. Now their bones lie on the bottom of the lake or have long since rotted away. Not a single cargo carrier from the lake's once vast fleet of commercial sail survives. Pollution and changing times have eliminated the rare lotus flowers, too, but thanks to caring owners and devoted volunteers the *Lotus* lives on. She was entered onto the National Register of Historic Places in 1990 and, in a few more years, hopefully will join the handful of wooden yachts on the lake that can claim a century of service.

The socioeconomic structure of yachting was highly stratified on early twentieth-century Lake Ontario (as elsewhere). The wealthy sailed aboard *Cangarda* or the 130-foot *Oriole*. They owned patent medicine companies or distilleries or fruit and vegetable canneries. The emerging middle class went adventuring aboard tiny sailboats like the little *Vivian*. They had some leisure time and spare money but not a lot of either. Credit cards and boat loans lay far in the future, as did paid vacations, so buying a boat back then was a cash proposition, and using it was mostly done on weekends. Not surprisingly, very early on, the middle-class lovers of yachting embraced the DIY approach, often building their own small boats from scratch. And a New York boating periodical was a major contributor to the early growth of budget boating.

In 1891, the *Rudder*, a journal of aquatic sport, began publication. The first issue bore on its masthead an engraved image of a small island typical of those found in the upper St. Lawrence resort area flanked by a sailing

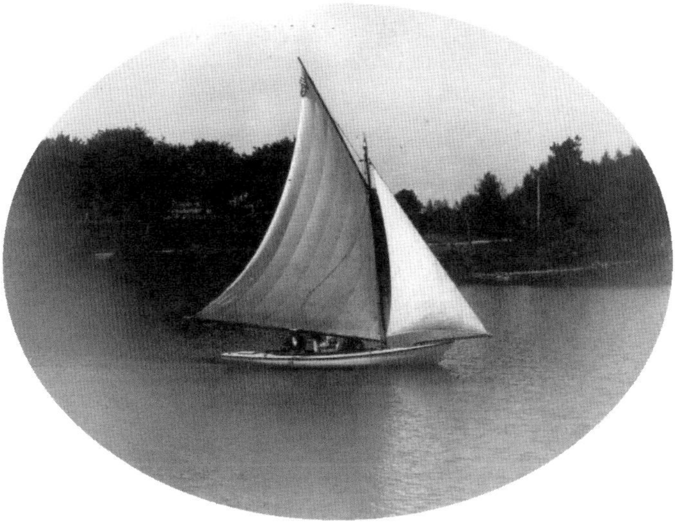

The log of the *Vivian* tells in verse of a memorable sail from Pultneyville to Sodus in 1899 by two young gentlemen of leisure. *Photo from Eleanor Fairbanks.*

skiff and a small power launch, probably no coincidence since the periodical was based in New York City, an overnight train away from the then popular vacation area. The *Rudder* soon became a national force for promoting middle-class boating in general and for the build-it-yourself ethic that went with it. It promoted power and sailboats, both types of boats benefited from a backyard building boom of the early to mid-twentieth century. However, space limits me to sailing craft.

In 1898, the *Rudder* published plans for building "Lark," a small, simple sailing scow. She was your basic box, with six inches of freeboard, a six-foot beam and sixteen-foot length. She had a single gaff sail, not unlike the wildly popular Sunfish and Sailfish sailboats of sixty years later. Thousands of these little one-design racers were built. The Rochester Canoe Club website mentions a fleet of fifteen boats built for the Sodus Bay Yacht Club at a cost of ninety dollars each in 1903. Many more were home built and were raced and sailed locally through the 1930s.

Building your own boat made it possible for the would-be captain to spread costs from one paycheck to the next. And by 1930, he could choose the size and complexity of his project, as there were hundreds of plans for boats ranging from ten-foot dinghies to forty-foot cruisers available. Before World War II,

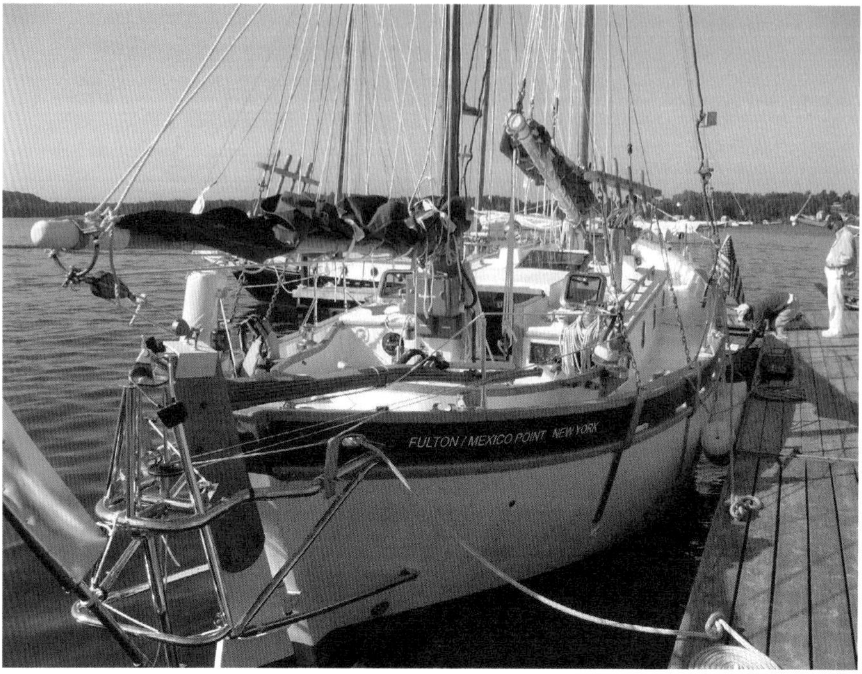

Ramsey's Dream, a wooden Tahiti ketch, built with nearly two decades of labor by the owner, typifies the get 'er done ethic of determined boat builders. *Author's collection.*

moderately priced lumberyard pine and hardwoods were suitable for many boat projects. After the war, good clear-grain, boat-building lumber became increasingly scarce and expensive, but plywood gave DIY boat building a new boost. After World War II, small arc welders also made steel amateur construction possible, and magazines began offering metal hull designs.

By the 1930s, a number of boat shops offered kits of precut parts that the basement or backyard builder could assemble using simple hand tools. The packing crate often set up as a jig to position the keel stem and transom. One company shipped more than ninety thousand boat kits between 1950 and 1958. This was a time when manual skills were still widespread. Many men knew how to use a hand plane or a chisel to work wood, and the pioneering skills of self-reliance and problem solving went well with DIY yachting. Even the Great Depression didn't slow the backyard builders down much.

In 1931, a boating magazine published plans for a little fifteen-foot sailboat, the *Snipe*. Her advent reflected the growing importance of the automobile to recreational activity of all sorts. *Snipe* was the first successful, widely built sailing-class designed to travel overland. She brought yachting (admittedly on a modest scale) to places where it had never before been.

At the time, trailer boating was in its infancy. One website says that, in 1939, only one thousand boat trailers were manufactured. Most boat trailers, like many boats of the time, were homemade. People scrounged old farm wagon axles, junk cars, pickup truck axles and the like to build their own. I remember one boat trailer in my early days of sailing equipped with heavy sidewall surplus tires from a World War II bomb cart.

Snipe came early to the Lake Ontario shore. Oak Orchard had a large and active fleet from the 1930s, as did Irondequoit and Sodus Bays. Back then, the estimated seasonal cost of owning a Snipe was thirty dollars, a goodly sum for quite a few people during the Great Depression. Syndicates to own small boats that split up the costs were common, as people figured out ways to sail on a shoestring.

In 1938, the Skaneateles Boat Company, builders of St. Lawrence Skiffs and several popular small sailboats like the Snipe and Comet, built the first nineteen-foot Lightning, a one-design sloop. One-design sailboats were raced in fleets at yacht and boat clubs. They were, at least in theory, all identical so that the race was won by skill rather than by equipment. The Lark was an early example.

The Barnes Brothers of Skaneateles wanted to offer a larger version of the sixteen-foot Comet—a boat with seats in which the whole family could sit comfortably. They commissioned a young but up-and-coming yacht designer, Olin Stephens, and built number one in late 1938. She was launched and test sailed on Skaneateles Lake by Olin Stephen's brother Rod on a blustery late fall day and was declared a success. Stephens signed the rights over to a class association and soon, even as the Skaneateles shop went into production, Lightning plans and kits were being purchased by amateur builders across the land. The little boats went on to become one of the most popular one-design racing classes of the twentieth century.

In the late 1950s, technology in the form of fiberglass again profoundly changed pleasure boating, and none too soon for middle-class sailors as centuries of relentless logging had pretty well cleaned out local supplies of decent boat timber in upstate New York (and elsewhere). Rising prices and reduced availability of lumber, along with wartime technology, brought about plastic boats, and some of the earliest experimentation took place on or near Lake Ontario.

Back in 1944, *Yachting* magazine ran an article on Corolite as a potential boat building material. It consisted of sheets of felted fiber impregnated with

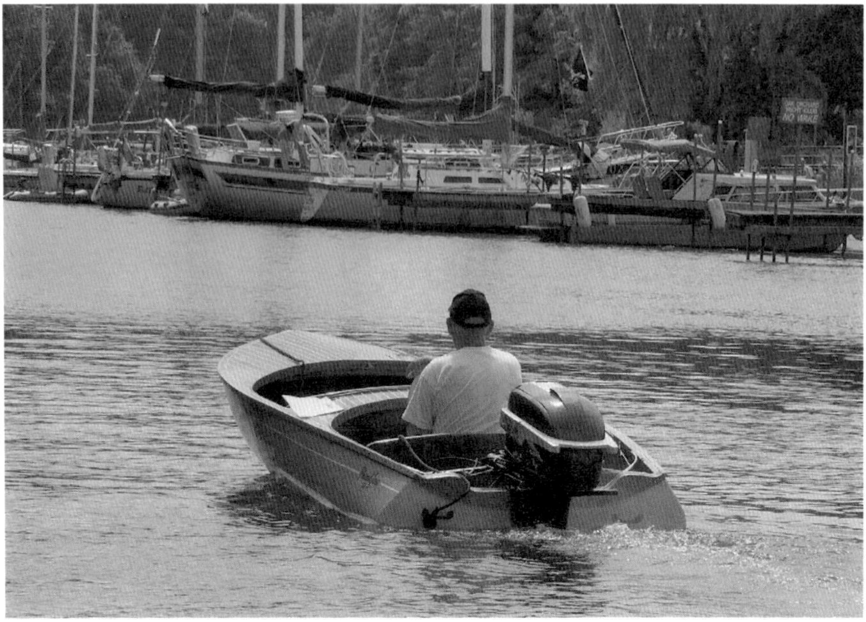

Upstate New York's Penn Yan Boats built sailing, rowing and power crafts. Its 1936 Car Topper resembled the Swift (shown here) and, like the Snipe, was designed for auto transport. *Author's collection.*

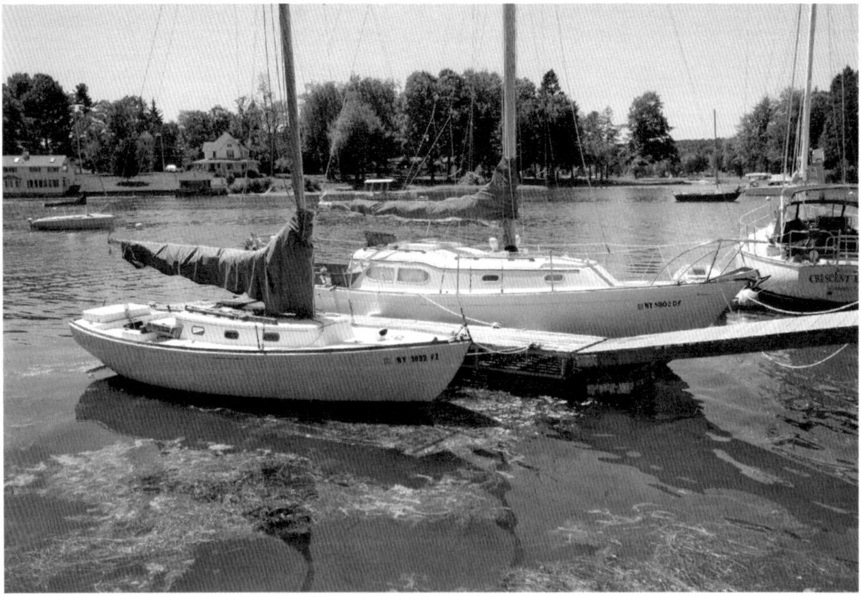

Two 1960s-era sloops, both designed by Olin Stephens, from the golden age of U.S. fiberglass boat production. *Author's collection.*

plastic resin that were laid up and "cooked" in a mold to create "jettison" fuel tanks for long-distance flights by observation planes and bombers. A couple of upstate yachters quickly recognized the material's potential and, in the summer of 1943, created a catamaran sailboat on Owasco Lake using two rejected tanks. The article stated, "When the Co-Ro-Cat was hauled out at the close of the season, there were no visible signs of deterioration, abrasion, or water absorption. This winter she is being stored outdoors, pontoons up, near the laboratory, where careful observation will be made of the effects of rain, snow, ice, and sunshine."

As soon as the war was over, people got serious about creating plastic boats. The advent of air-cured resins that didn't need to be cooked made plastic hulls far more feasible, and by 1947, a small fiberglass day sailor was displayed at the New York Boat Show. In the late 1950s, a Canadian boat builder on the shores of Lake Ontario began offering fiberglass sailboats, the most successful of which was a peppy little racer, the twenty-four-foot Shark still widely sailed today. The Hinterholler shop later merged with another very successful Canadian firm, C&C Yachts. They claim in 1965 to have launched the first balsa-cored hull, a forty-foot racer named *Red Jacket*.

Like the earlier DIY movement, fiberglass made boats more affordable. The labor to build a plastic boat was considerably less than what was involved to craft a wooden hull. Hulls were laid up in molds, so most builders did production runs of multiple identical hulls to save time. And the maintenance involved in keeping a plastic boat water tight and functional was a fraction of that needed for an older wooden boat. The 1960s and '70s were a boom time for sailing on Lake Ontario as a wealth of affordable plastic boats was available then.

But plastic also changed the collective character of the boats used. Previously shops often built boats adapted to local waters, like the St. Lawrence Skiff. Shallow areas called for shallow-draft boats. Windy places required sturdy vessels with less sail area and deeper keels with ballast. But the production glass boats homogenized the yachting scene, and diverse regional types soon were pushed aside by plastic hulls. Some sailors who value heritage and tradition feel this is a loss. Yet because the durable fiberglass boats last for so long, acquiring a yacht has never been more affordable. Though many are nearly fifty years old, plastic boats appear to be going strong. Comparable traditionally built wooden boats with galvanized fastenings would have been expected to last twenty years in the 1930s.

Yachting on the lake through the years has reflected the larger history of our nation. The *Cangarda* was financed initially with wealth generated from natural resources of the Great Lakes region at a time when smokestack industries dominated the area. She was rebuilt with West Coast money generated by a globalized business in finance. *Lotus*, once the plaything of leisured upstate sailors, now takes youngsters out of the house and onto the lake, far from video games and iPods, where they can connect with the natural world. No one could have foreseen the need for that when she was launched more than ninety years ago.

CHAPTER 8

LAKE ONTARIO'S LEGENDARY TRIO

Many fish stories have been told about the ancient one, the leaper and the far traveler—the legendary Lake Ontario trio. The oldest of them, literally, is the sturgeon. A deliberate and patient forager, sturgeons can endure sometimes for over a century in the lake's depths. The shining silver salmon is held in high regard by European and First Nation peoples alike, and the American eel even today remains a fish of mystery. After a century of scientific study, no one yet knows where the eel is born or where it goes to die.

THE ANCIENT ONE

The Great Lakes sturgeon, if for no other reason, would be a legend today simply because of its size. These days, they are also rare, and during a half century of lake watching, I have seen the great fish only once. I was a child of six or seven visiting a lakeshore neighbor's house on a cool, breezy May afternoon with my mother for a women's church group picnic. Bored by the proceedings, I wandered over to the edge of the low bluff to look at the water. Below, in the surf that washed over a wide shelf of rock, I saw a dozen huge brown fish. They were thrashing and flailing to and fro in the surf. I stared at the fishy mêlée in a mix of childish fascination and fear. These monsters were way bigger than I was. They looked like they were trying to crawl out of the lake. I thought they were, perhaps, dying. I ran back to the picnic table hollering about the big fish. I probably said something about them coming ashore to eat me or something else as equally perceptive. "Oh, they're sturgeon; they're just laying their eggs," the hostess reassured me.

At the time, I was about four feet tall, and some of those fish were easily twice my size. Since then, I have watched in vain for them. I long to see them again now, a half century later, but as yet, I have only watched them glide around in aquarium and fish hatchery tanks.

One record-sized lake sturgeon caught many years ago was nine feet long and weighed over 390 pounds. Fish weighing 200 to 300 pounds were relatively common in the early 1800s on the lake. Slow-growing sturgeon are known to have lived over a century in captivity. I once viewed an aquarium specimen that was estimated to be 150 years old. She would have been a youngster mooching around for worms when Lincoln was shot. (Like the American eel, female sturgeon get bigger and live longer than males.) Sturgeon are bottom feeders and live primarily on small clams, leeches and worms found in the mud of the inshore depths. Young fish favor insect larvae and small invertebrates. They occasionally also eat a round goby or two, but fish are not a big part of their diet. Sturgeon have four whiskers, or "barbels," somewhat like those of the catfish, on their nose. These help them smell food, as they use their long snouts to stir up the mud and silt. They then suck up the tidbits. They don't have teeth despite their vaguely shark-shaped look, a reflection of their ancient heritage.

I once assisted in a study of short-nosed sturgeon in the Connecticut River. They proved to be exceptionally docile and placid when pulled into the boat for measuring, weighing and tagging. The lake sturgeon also, by all accounts, is a harmless fish, despite its formidable appearance and my childhood impressions.

The ancient one has been gliding around in salt and freshwater shallows for at least 200 million years, long before the reign of the dinosaurs. In Lake Ontario, only the lamprey eel, which is so primitive it doesn't even have jaws, has an older origin. The sturgeon has been called a "living fossil," thanks to the boney armor of platelike "scutes" along its back and sides and its sharklike tail and head. The sturgeon is so ancient that part of its internal skeleton is made of cartilage rather than bone, and it lacks the conventional vertebrate backbone of more modern fish, having instead a structure of cartilage called a notocord. The armor plates help protect young sturgeon from predators and recall the fish's ancestry of armor-plated fishes from the Devonian era 350 million years go that eventually gave rise to the two main branches of today's finny folk—sharks and boney fishes.

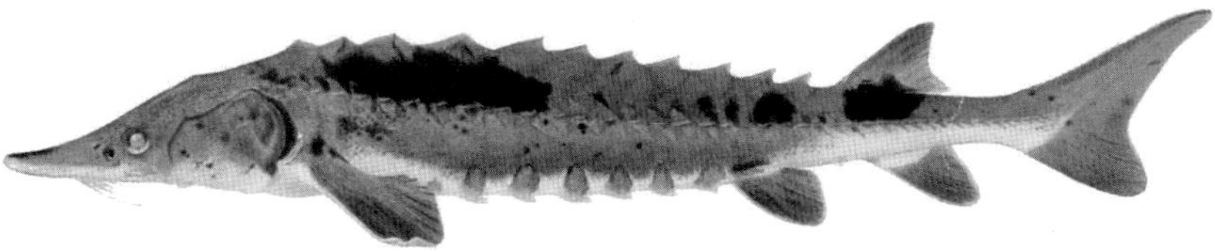

The sharklike appearance of the sturgeon reflects its ancient heritage. They grew to over six feet in days past. *Wikipedia commons.*

Sturgeon were found throughout the Great Lakes and were once common in Lake Ontario. The lower St. Lawrence still has a fairly viable population. (In 1996, about two hundred metric tons were harvested commercially from the Quebec portion of the river.) Surprisingly, this source of prized caviar and high-quality flesh was regarded as a trash fish in the early 1800s. Big, slow sturgeon lumbering along the bottom would get tangled up in nets set for perch or bullhead and would then thrash their way out, tearing up and tangling the gear as they did so. Because no local market then existed for caviar, they were often killed and dumped back in the lake. There are tales of sturgeon being hauled out and stacked on shore to dry. Their bodies were then burned as fuel in steamer boilers. Other early accounts of the Lake Ontario fishery record sturgeon being fed to pigs or used as fertilizer on the fields.

The native peoples, however, prized the oily fleshed sturgeon, whose meat was well suited to smoking, drying and salting. Mishe-Nahme, the king of fishes, as Longfellow calls the sturgeon in the "Song of Hiawatha," was a vital part of their diet throughout the region. They built weirs of stone in rivers to divert and concentrate the fish as they traveled upstream to spawn. The Seneca Band used large rakes to drive them into the weir "pocket," where they could then spear them. Other Indian bands harpooned them from canoes, according to Charlevoix. Their bone harpoon heads have been found in considerable numbers at sites around Chaumont Bay as well as by the outlets of Oneida Lake at Brewerton and at Onondaga Lake. In New England, the Indians used torches to light up the shallows at night and attract the sturgeon inshore to be speared. It seems likely tribes here sometimes used similar techniques.

Lafitau in the Jesuit Relations recalled, "The meat of the sturgeon [and the eel and the salmon] was preserved by smoking. During the summer, they [the lodges] are cool enough, but full of fleas and bedbugs, and stink very badly when they [the Indians] dry their fish in the smoke."

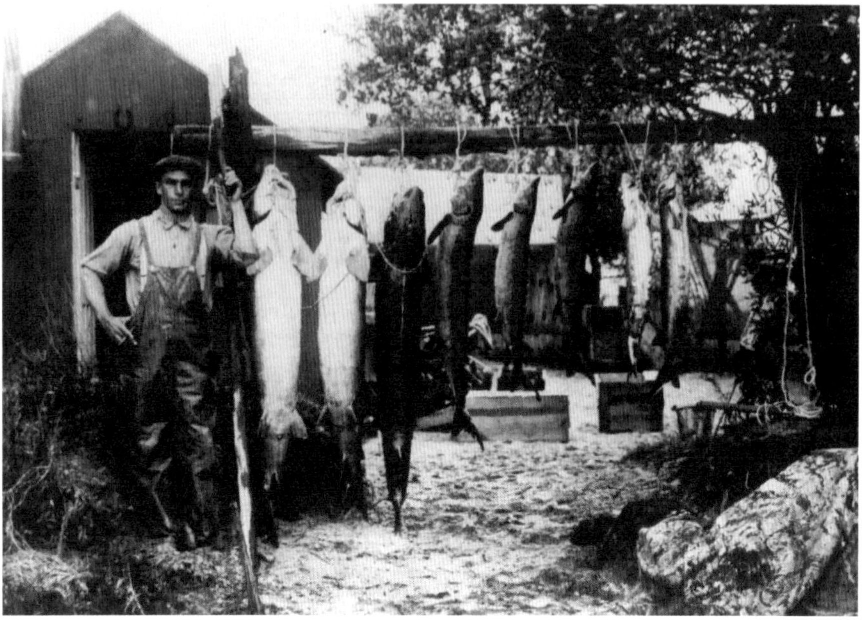

This photo, taken around 1930, shows clearly the effects of unsustainable fishing. The smaller sturgeon have probably never spawned. *Photo from Bill Huff.*

By the 1870s, the Europeans were beginning to share the Iroquois' views of the sturgeon. After the advent of rail, it was possible to quickly move goods to distant markets. This brought about the rise of large-scale commercial fishing, and increasingly, the once scorned sturgeon was sought after for its firm, oily flesh and for a material called isinglass that was made from dried swim bladders. Among its other uses, isinglass was used by brewers to accelerate the clarification of beer. By the 1920s, in harbors like Pultneyville and Sodus Bay, the fish were being caught on trotlines and held in pens until enough were on hand for a butchering day. Then the iced fish were transported to the rail station and taken to downstate markets.

After commercial fishing for them began, the sturgeon population quickly dwindled. These long-lived fish grow slowly and often don't begin to reproduce until age twenty or more. Thereafter, they spawn only every few years. Sometimes, females spawn only once in nine years. Though a large fish may produce half a million eggs, the vast majority of these offspring are either eaten before hatching or gobbled up as tiny fish by predators. Infant sturgeon grow quickly, though, and can reach seven inches or more in size after a year. The juveniles are then, with their hard bony surface armor, big enough to escape most predators.

Dams and pollution were two other major contributors to the population decline. Many populations of fish moved up rivers like the Oswego and Genesee to spawn. When they were blocked by dams, the clean-flowing water and gravel bottom needed for egg survival were no longer available to them. The fish that spawned in the open lake also had to contend with changes in the shoreline habitat. As pollution from sewage and other sources added nutrients to the lake, seaweed (of the filamentous algae genus called *Chladophora*) began to cover the rocks with a dense growth that may have suffocated the deposited eggs. The little remaining river habitat for spawning or for nursery areas available below dams was often degraded by dredging and additional pollution.

Any fish that escaped natural hazards were eagerly sought by fishermen. In the 1920s, a major source of caviar for European markets was our own lake sturgeon. Today, smoked sturgeon goes for $65 a pound, so a one-hundred-pound fish adds up to real money. Caviar, the unspawned salted eggs of the sturgeon, recently was selling for $2,500 a pound, according to one website. Poaching is a big problem worldwide, and one recent scientific study of St. Lawrence River sturgeon spawning had an *X* over the location, presumably to protect the vulnerable fish from illegal spearing or netting.

There is no fishing season now for sturgeon on Lake Ontario, and a few populations hang on here. Sturgeon are sighted regularly in the Niagara River area, and a couple tributaries of the St. Lawrence also have regular spawning runs. Surveys and sightings suggest that these populations are stable or possibly even increasing. In the 1990s, a variety of federal state partnerships got underway to develop sturgeon recovery plans. Efforts began in New York in 1994 with fish being stocked in waters that were their historic homes, including Oneida Lake, Black Lake, Cayuga Lake, the St. Lawrence River and several tributaries, such as the St. Regis. Within a few years, angler sightings and incidental catches were on the upswing throughout the state. For the first time in fifty years, the future began to look a bit brighter for this most ancient and enduring of the lake's fish.

In the fall of 2003 and 2004, a total of 1,900 juvenile sturgeon eight to ten inches long were released in the lower Genesee River. Initial follow-up surveys suggested good survival and growth as the young fish favored deeper areas of the river with gravel and mud bottom. They hoovered up midge larvae from the mud at a great rate and, as they grew, tended to wander northward toward the open lake. In 2009, one tagged three-foot youngster was found in the river that weighed ten pounds. The study results note that, in 2020, the first spawning run could occur. One wonders if any funding will then be available to look for them. As the report notes, the length of the study exceeds that of many scientists' careers. Perhaps I will drive to Charlotte some May afternoon, if I'm still around, with the hope of seeing a free-swimming sturgeon as I once did a half century ago.

The Leaper

Probably no Lake Ontario fish has more charisma and appeal than the strong silver salmon as it bursts from the water in a spectacular leap when ascending a stream to spawn. Its very name is derived from the Latin word *salirer*, "to leap," and the leaper it is. Salmon surmount formidable obstacles in their relentless reproductive drive to their spawning redds. A study of steelhead (near relatives of the Atlantic salmon) found them able to get past a cascade that had a drop of twelve feet over a thirty-seven-foot horizontal distance.

Most Atlantic salmon spend much of their lives in salt water and then return home to the stream where they were born to spawn. After the young fish hatch, they stay in the stream feeding on insects and insect larvae until they are a few inches long. Then, the "parr," as they're called, begin to work their way downstream to salt water, where they mature over a period of several years. A number of salmon populations, however, are landlocked, such as those of Lake Ontario, and they adapt readily to spending their whole lives in fresh water.

The sleek, bright-sided salmon has long fascinated people. The ancient Celts considered it to be the fish of knowledge. A story told in Ireland and Wales tells that a salmon devoured nine hazelnuts that fell from nine trees around the well of wisdom in which it swam. The fish gained all of the world's wisdom and was able to pass that on to whoever ate it. The Scandinavians admired salmon for their strength and determination, as they swam against the current in a sometimes lengthy quest to reach the spawning grounds far from the sea.

Atlantic salmon once ran up streams to spawn throughout Europe, with a range that extended as far south as Portugal, so the fish was familiar to the early explorers who came to the lakeshore in the 1600s. Like the sturgeon and eel, it was also an important part of the First Nation peoples' diets,

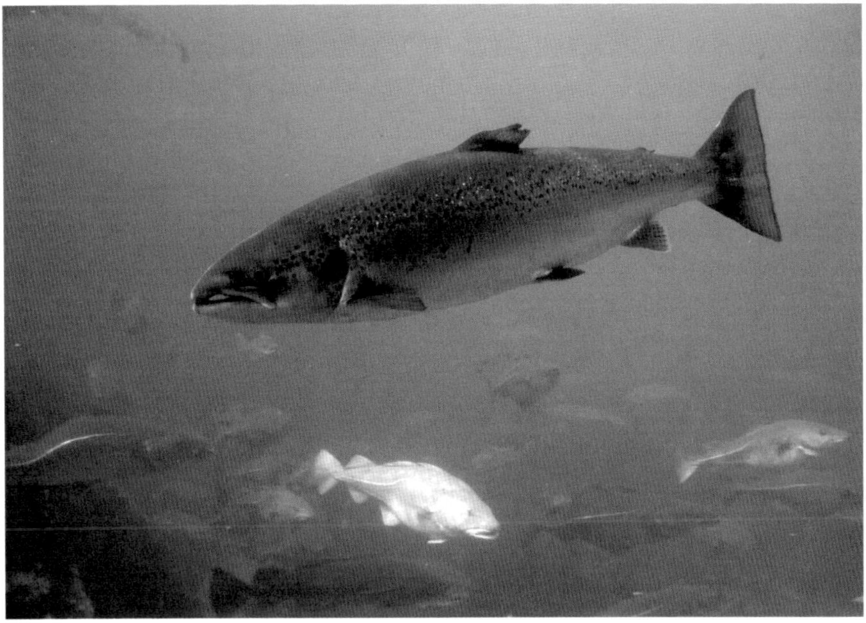

Strong-swimming salmon can travel hundreds of miles to reach their spawning grounds. *Photo from Wikipedia commons.*

but the salmon doesn't seem to have had quite the spiritual importance for them that it had for the northern Europeans. Before 1800, fish weighing up to forty-five pounds were found in the lake. The largest record for a North American angler catch is said to be sixty-four pounds, while hundred-pound sea-run fish have showed up in fishing nets. There almost certainly were forty- to sixty-pound fish here in colonial days.

Sadly, however, despite the esteem that European settlers held for it, the salmon did not fare well in North America after their arrival. Today, the native Lake Ontario strain of Atlantic salmon is extinct. Worldwide salmon populations are also in decline, and attempts to restore our shining native leaper face formidable obstacles thanks to profound changes in the lake's food web and watershed.

Once Lake Ontario, some say, was the greatest salmon lake in the world. Early tales of runs include four hundred fish averaging fifteen pounds each speared by one man in one night. On another night, two thousand fish were speared during a run on the Salmon River. Other stories tell of runs so heavy and close packed that farmers stood in the water and pitchforked the fish onto the shore or scooped them up with bushel baskets.

An early settler built a dam and mill on Red Creek in Wayne County. He also served as the Methodist preacher for the village. Once, on his way to church on a fine summer Sunday morning around 1820, he looked down into the creek below his dam. At this time, no other structures blocked the fish run, so the salmon could get as far as the dam. When he saw the mass of silvery fish crowded below the barrier, he hurried home to tell his sons, "I've just seen a fine shoal of large salmon down by the mill; but it is Sunday, and you must not take them on Sunday." The boys, so the account goes, decided their father had misspoken, using the word "not" by mistake, so they skipped church, and "there was a dreadful slaughter of salmon and a nice fish bake for Sunday dinner."

Because they were highly sought after and so vulnerable during the spawning runs, the salmon population, like those of so many other fishes of Lake Ontario, dwindled rapidly. Most authorities believe that along with overfishing, huge changes in the watershed spelled their doom. In 1820, much of the lakeshore was heavily forested, and streams ran cool and clear year-round. The salmon, like our native brook trout, is a fish of the forest. It needs cool, fast-running water with high oxygen content. But by 1870, the trees had been cleared, and much of the landscape was under cultivation or was being used as pasture.

Precipitation that once had soaked slowly into deep forest soils to feed springs and woodland creeks now ran off quickly. Springs that had once flowed year-round dried up. This, along with the relentless extermination of the beaver, greatly changed the flow and character of shoreline streams. Many were now too warm, too silty or ceased to flow in the summer. And by the 1870s, no more deep, shaded pools behind beaver dams existed for the young fish to shelter in as the beavers had all been trapped out or starved for lack of forest forage.

Man-made dams, various mills and tanneries and other hydro-powered industries also blocked the spawning runs and polluted the water. Log drives down rivers in the spring scoured and impacted the gravel bottom needed for spawning and increased the suffocating mud and silt entering the streams from erosion. After the Civil War, less than 25 percent of New York State remained forested, and most of that was in the Adirondacks and the Catskills. Lack of good spawning grounds, along with overfishing, pollution, dams and possibly the accidental introduction of two small baitfish in the lake, spelled the end for the lake's leaper. The native Atlantic salmon was gone from Lake Ontario by 1890. Green wrote in his history of Sodus Bay that the salmon was once very numerous in Second Creek just west of Thornton Point, but "as there were no game laws in those days, it was taken in great numbers by the people of the region." He added that their numbers rapidly decreased and that one Nate May of Sodus Point speared two in the creek in the 1850s. Those, he wrote, were the last of their kind ever seen or taken there. A fish that had roamed Lake Ontario's depths for thousands of years disappeared within a long human lifetime.

Sporadic efforts were made through the years to establish various salmon and other trout species in the lake by stocking. All failed, thanks largely to lamprey predation and polluted dam-blocked tributaries. In the early 1970s, however, a successful lamprey control program for Lake Ontario's tributaries was begun and the population of parasites reduced. The United States and Canada then developed a joint plan to restore the lake's important lake trout fishery and to introduce several nonnative West Coast salmon species. The hope was that they would eat up the excess alewives, that were then making a nuisance of themselves by dying on the beaches, while also creating a trophy fishery. Today, Lake Ontario's sport fishery brings tens of millions of dollars of economic activity and thousands of anglers to the region as hungry Pacific salmon species gobble up the baitfish.

Fish tales are again being told about giant silvery fish that got away. But few of them are Atlantic salmon. It appears that our native salmon doesn't do well on a diet of smelt and alewife. These two small baitfish are not Lake Ontario natives, having been either accidentally or, in some places, intentionally introduced from saltwater some years ago. They have replaced the native lake herring and chubs that were once the major food of adult Atlantic salmon, and a heavy diet of them appears to affect the salmon's ability to absorb the vitamin Thiamine (vitamin B1), a nutrient that is vital to their health and reproduction. An enzyme called thiaminase, found in both alewife and smelt, breaks the vitamin down before the salmon can store it. Recent studies suggest that the types of food the alewife and smelt eat may influence the amount of vitamin-destroying enzyme they produce. Since the lake's food web is constantly being rearranged with new alien species being introduced frequently, it's hard to predict how events may play out. But for the time being, the future for Lake Ontario's only native salmon is bleak. Most that are caught by anglers today are the result of the releases of hatchery-raised fish since the free ranging Atlantics no longer seem to produce viable eggs and larvae.

At the lake's east end, clear, cool-running streams and rivers, such as the Black and Salmon Rivers and Orwell Creek, do furnish suitable spawning for a limited number of Atlantic salmon; however, even if they could deal with an alewife diet, competition from other stocked trout and salmon species would probably prevent them from successful spawning. It seems likely that we will never again see them crowd into streams so close packed that the hungry fisherman could simply pluck one from the water bare handed.

The Eel

The incredible American eel lacks the charisma of the gleaming silver salmon or the huge lumbering sturgeon, though it has been called the world's most mysterious fish. Many people confuse eels with the "blood sucking" sea lamprey in Lake Ontario. And both the snakelike eel and the lamprey are generally viewed as slimy and repulsive. One online resource described the adaptable eel's food habits, which includes eating dead fish (a food preference it shares with the bald eagle), as "disgusting." But no other fish makes a journey like that of the far-traveling eel. Among all the lake's fishes, only the eel goes to sea to reproduce. Scientists believe that all the humble little brown eels in Lake Ontario that reach maturity make a one-way voyage to the distant deep blue Sargasso Sea to spawn and then die. But no one has actually seen one do it.

A number of non-European cultures, including the Iroquois, have held the eel in high esteem, even believing it to be a sacred being. On some Polynesian Islands, the resident freshwater eel population is held to be a shaper of fate and human destiny. Stories of "Tuna," a god who assumed the form of a large eel, are widespread. In one version, he sacrifices himself to prevent a great flood. In another, after his death, the first coconut tree springs from his head. (On many South Seas islands the coconut's rich meat was the staff of life itself, utterly essential to the islanders' survival.) On some islands today, tourists feed these sacred eels canned mackerel presumably from properly consecrated cans. Ambon Island in Indonesia has a spring with sacred (or at least lucky) eels that happily chow down on eggs given to them by admirers.

The pre-colonial residents of the lakeshore included the Onondagas, who number the Eel Clan among their five tribal clans. The eel, with its rich oily flesh, was, like the sturgeon, well suited to smoking, and the Longhouse people relied heavily on it for their winter supplies of food. Around 1650, one of the scribes contributing to the Jesuit Relations recorded, "The eel constitutes a manna exceeding all belief. Experience and ingenuity have

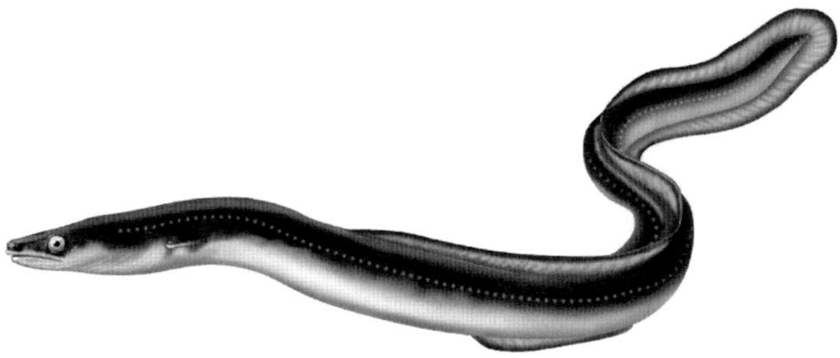

Lake Ontario's eels may travel nearly four thousand miles to reach the Sargasso Sea. *Author's collection.*

rendered us so expert at catching them that one or two men will take 5 or 6000 in a single night; And this fishing lasts for two whole months in which an ample provision of them is made for the whole year, for the eels here have excellent qualities for keeping whether dried by fire or salted and are much better than any eels in France." The tribes built weirs of stone or brush to trap eels during their downstream runs in the fall or they speared them from canoes at night by torch light.

Europeans in the nineteenth century also prized the eel, and commercial fisheries using pots, trot lines and eel weirs continued into the 1900s on Lake Ontario and inland waters. The fish were generally salted and smoked for transport to distant markets. After capture, fish were split, salted and hung over the smokehouse fire. Most were "hot smoked"—cooked over a quick fire of corn cobs that was then converted to a "slow smudge" for up to fifteen hours. An account of the local industry in 1915 noted that adding sulfur to the fire produced a "rich brown color that greatly aids the sale." Back then, the average weight of an eel was about four pounds, and the smoked fish went for about twenty cents a pound in the fish market (roughly equivalent to four dollars a pound in today's currency).

Among Lake Ontario fish, only the sturgeon lives longer than the eel. In Germany, an eel kept in an aquarium lived for 88 years, and there is at least one unverified Internet reference to an eel that lived in a well for 130 years. Lake Ontario's eels don't reproduce until sometime between age twenty and fifty. All of our eels are female, for the mothers of the eel race are the largest and farthest traveled. Most eels found in brackish water or in coastal salt water are smaller males. As historic accounts suggest, eels were once very abundant here. They may have made up a third of all the lake's inshore fish population by weight.

They are hardy fish and can breathe through their skin if need be. During my fisheries career, more than once I found perfectly healthy small eels in the damp corners of our boat twenty-four hours after a sampling session. And I once saw a huge old eel crawl out of a pond that had been poisoned to get rid of the so-called trash fish. Reports exist that eels regularly forage ashore for worms and slugs on damp nights. Eels are termed generalists by the ecologists, meaning they can adapt to many different environments, including degraded ones. They do very well in warm, weedy shallows but also, at least formerly, manage just fine in the open lake's depths. I heard tales of spearing them at night by flashlight behind Eagle Island on Sodus Bay years ago, and in the 1990s, while walking on the Sodus jetty at dusk, a friend and I saw a number of big old ladies sticking their heads out from between the rocks and beginning to prowl around the riprap next to the pier. Eels work the night shift, which is one reason not many people know much about them. An online reference to animal totems states that the mysterious eel is associated with intuition. If you dream of the far-traveling eel, it may be a sign that your creative life is ready for a new direction.

In keeping with the general mystery about eels, we don't even know for certain how they determine their sex. Some studies suggest that, when there are dense populations of eels, the fish tend to be male. When there are fewer fish, more females result. We do know that virtually all the eels in Lake Ontario are female. One scientist, John Casselman of Queens University, writes that as much as half the production of the continent's entire stock of eels may have been contributed by Lake Ontario and St. Lawrence fish.

They eat pretty much anything they can catch while they live here: insect larvae, worms and fish alive or recently dead. Sometimes, they eat smaller eels. Then, after many years of mundane settled life wiggling around the ledges off Swetman Island or in Sodus Bay's weed beds, there comes a time of change for the eel. She begins to transform into a "silver." Her color changes from brown and yellow to silver and black, and she grows increasingly oily and fat. Her pectoral fins become long and pointed, and her eyes enlarge as her digestive track shrinks; she ceases to feed. Then one fall night something, no one knows exactly what, tells her it is time. Often it's a rainy night, and the silver eels catch a lift from the seaward flows of rain-swollen tributaries. Sometimes huge numbers of eels move downstream during a brief period of moonless nights. Perhaps half a century after her arrival, our Lake Ontario eel sets forth on a journey of many months' duration—down the

St. Lawrence to the Sargasso Sea, 3,700 miles away, somewhere south and east of Bermuda.

How she finds her way is yet uncertain. Tagged European eels tracked by telemetry varied their depth from near surface at night down to three thousand feet during the day as they traveled. They may have used currents or gotten an energy boost from the warm shallows or even used stars at night for navigation. One Norwegian study showed that eels in a laboratory tank oriented to varied magnetic fields. Perhaps as they swim south, they regulate the development of eggs and sperm by varying the time spent in deep cold water so that they all synchronize when they at last meet up somewhere in the ocean's depths.

No one yet knows for certain how the eels all make their way to the exact location of the open-ocean spawning grounds, where a mass orgy produces the next generation of eels. We do know they have an extremely good sense of smell. Several studies suggest eels use their noses in part to find their way to sea or to return to home territories after scientists move them. One study of European eels found the young elvers could tell what type of bottom the water they were exposed to had flowed over. So perhaps when they near the spawning ground, their noses know where to go.

It requires vast endurance to reach the distant spawning grounds, and scientists who have analyzed eel energetics say that the larger eels produced by northern waters such as Lake Ontario have higher fat reserves and a definite edge as they transport themselves and their millions of eggs to their rendezvous with the males. Somewhere in the dark depths of the Sargasso they meet and spawn, and the next generation hatches as tiny transparent ribbonlike larvae that look nothing at all like an eel. For a long time, people thought they were a different species of fish altogether and called them leptocephali.

The infant eels ride the Gulf Stream northward and somehow distribute themselves to the various tributaries and bays of the East and Gulf Coasts. (Again, nobody knows exactly how they manage to sort themselves out.

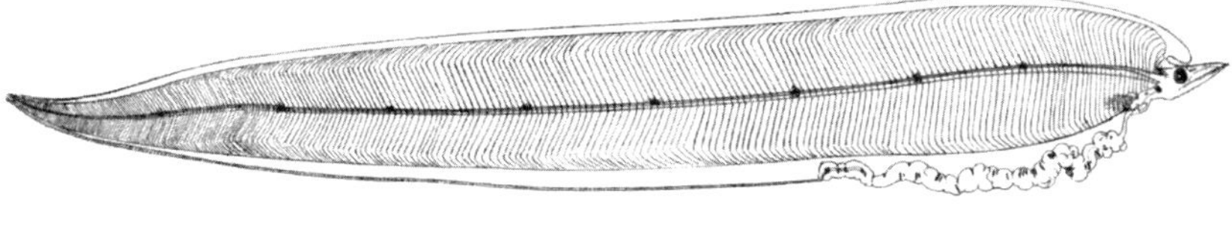

Despite the leptocephali's delicate appearance, these odd little fish are efficient swimmers and are well able to elude researchers' plankton nets. *Wikimedia commons.*

It's believed that eels do not home to the waters from which their parents originated.) A few go as far south as Venezuela. Some go all the way north to Greenland. And one web page states that genetically distinct American eels have even turned up in Europe. Europe's eels seem to be a separate species but spawn in the same area as Lake Ontario's fish. Somehow, they sort themselves out, and our lake eels arrive at the St. Lawrence after several years of travel. En route between salt water and the upper St. Lawrence, they turn into "glass eels" and then grow to become darkly colored six-inch elvers. Historically, vast swarms of baby eels ascended the river in spring and early summer. They were so numerous that an observer wrote he caught over five hundred with a few grabs of his bare hands.

This was the pattern for thousands of years on Lake Ontario. Then, fifty years ago, about the life span of the lake's oldest and biggest eels, something changed. The St. Lawrence Seaway opened, and the Moses Saunders Power Dam went into operation. In 1985, more than a million elvers climbed the dam's fish ladder at its north end. Fifteen years later, virtually no baby eels appeared there. Lake Ontario's eel population had crashed in a sudden collapse that stunned the scientific community. While various reasons for the crash were put forth, ranging from overfishing to chemical pollutants affecting the long-lived fish, a prime suspect was the dam. All the river's flow goes through it. There is no bypass. So all the lake's eels must go through it too. Studies suggest that up to 40 percent of the eels running downstream to the sea were being killed outright as they passed through the power turbines. Unfortunately, the biggest, most fecund fish were the most likely not to make it through. And no one knows how many more were injured but still able to swim away. Even a slight wound would almost certainly impact an eel's chances of completing her long, grueling journey to the Sargasso. Studies of eels moving to the sea in Maine suggest power dam turbines there may kill up to 90 percent of the fish.

And it wasn't just our eels that were in trouble. Fisheries in Northern Europe, Japan and the Mediterranean were also in catastrophic decline. In Europe, elvers were at 5 percent of their 1980s' numbers. And in Japan, where eels are a national dish, millions are being spent on eel farm research as wild-caught eels vanish. In 2003, at a conference in Quebec, scientists from eighteen countries drafted a "Declaration of Concern" regarding the embattled eels. Among other things, it said, "Recruitment of the Lake Ontario population has virtually ceased." The number of baby eels coming into the system was less than 1 percent of the 1970 numbers seen. "Time was running out" for the lake's eels, the researchers concluded.

Even as various scientific conferences urged action to no avail, two brothers on the East Coast launched a citizens' petition in late 2004 requesting that the eel be listed under the Endangered Species Act. Theirs was a true jousting at windmills as they took on the vast federal bureaucracy. The effort gained national press coverage (perhaps because of its human interest angle of two odd ball guys who cared about slimy, nasty eels). Three years later, in 2007, after reams of paper work, tens of thousands of words, much foot dragging and finally a lawsuit filed on behalf of the brothers to prod the government into action, the Fish and Wildlife Service declared an endangered listing for the eel was "not warranted."

One of the petitioners, Doug Watts, noted that the status review to determine the eel's potential for extinction failed utterly to consider the "cumulative effects" of all the problems the eel was faced with—dams, overfishing, toxic pollutants, newly introduced blood-sucking parasites that have the potential to critically weaken the eels as they undertake their long journeys and even possible shifting ocean currents due to climate change. He noted that a similar review of the status of the Atlantic salmon ran three hundred pages while that for the eel, with its incredibly complex and far-ranging life cycle, was just thirty pages. It was, in the view of the eel supporters, a token document, filed strictly to fulfill legal obligations under the Endangered Species Act. Perhaps one of the most curious assumptions that the status review included was that eels didn't need freshwater habitat. It cited studies showing female eels can reach maturity in salt water or in estuaries like the Chesapeake. This may be true, but nobody knows how often they do so. Will there be enough of them to complete the long journey and find their fellow fishes in the far reaches of the Sargasso? Some eel scientists question the assumption that there will be.

In 2010, the Council for Endangered Species Act Reliability (CESAR), a nonprofit legal group with a mission of bringing "scientific rigor to regulatory decisions," filed a second petition on behalf of the eel, requesting "threatened" status citing new information that had not been available at the time of the first finding. The nonprofit also cited the inadequacy of existing "regulatory mechanisms" for the protection of the eel. In part, the petition stated, "It is unconscionable that a resource agency charged with regulatory responsibility for a resource could exist in near total ignorance of the status of that resource for decades." In the fall of 2011, the Department of the Interior finally responded by saying, "Petition presents substantial scientific or commercial information indicating that listing this species [as threatened] may be warranted." But still nothing happened. No action is a decision of sorts it seems, so CESAR followed the petition up in August 2012 with a lawsuit charging that agencies with authority to regulate under the law had failed to do so. The paper pushing goes on even as the eel numbers dwindle. Meanwhile, in Canada in 2007, the eel was classified as endangered.

There are things that could be done to help the American eel. Hydro dams could be shut down during the brief period of silver eel migration, and bypasses around the dams for the seaward-bound eels could be built. Fishing pressure could be reduced, and all fishing for the tiny glass eels (bringing over $2,000 a pound for export to Japanese eel farms in 2012) could be suspended. And the fisheries for adult eels could be restricted or eliminated. None of this is likely to happen in the United States, however, without some official change in the eel's legal status.

Eels are tough. They have been around since the time when Pangeia split apart to form Europe, the Americas and the Atlantic Ocean. They survived the great extinction of the Cretaceous period, when the dinosaurs died out, and a number of ice ages, too. But can the amazing eel survive humanity? Henry Beston wrote, "We need another and a wiser and perhaps a more mystical concept of animals…They are not brethren, they are not underlings; they are other nations, caught with ourselves within the net of life and time, fellow prisoners of the splendor and travail of the earth."

And so the battle for the future of the eel goes on.

SOURCES AND FURTHER READING

Beck, Horace. *Folklore and the Sea*. Mystic, CT: Mystic Seaport Museum, 1970

Cochrane, Hugh. *Gateway to Oblivion: The Great Lakes Bermuda Triangle*. New York: Doubleday, 1980.

Connors, John. *Pettiness in Paradise and Other Tales of Appleboom Point*. Bloomington, IN: Trafford, 2007.

Gateley, Susan Peterson *Ariadne's Death: Tales of Heroism and Tragedy*. Wolcott, NY: Whiskey Hill Press, 2006.

———. *Passages on Inland Waters*. Wolcott, NY: Whiskey Hill Press, 2004.

———. *Twinkle Toes and the Riddle of the Lake*. Wolcott, NY: Whiskey Hill Press, 2009.

Green, Walter Henry. *History, Reminiscences, Anecdotes and Legends of Great Sodus Bay*. Privately printed, 1947.

Merrill, Arch. "The Ridge Ontario's Blossom Country." *Democrat and Chronicle*, 1944.

Schneider, Stephen. *Iced: The Story of Organized Crime in Canada*. Hoboken, NJ: Wiley, 2009.

Tirrell, Art. *The Secret Ever Keeps*. N.p.: Kunati, 2007

WEBSITES

International Centre for Waterspout Research (ICWR), http://www.icwr.ca.

Lake Ontario Log, http://silverwaters.com/page3.htm.

ABOUT THE AUTHOR

Susan Peterson Gateley sails and writes on Lake Ontario. She has a science background and worked as a fisheries biologist and high school science teacher before taking up writing and publishing. Find her online at www.silverwaters.com.

OTHER BOOKS BY SUSAN PETERSON GATELEY

Living on the Edge with Sara B (Whiskey Hill Press, 2012)
Twinkle Toes and the Riddle of the Lake (Whiskey Hill Press, 2009)
Ariadne's Death Heroism and Tragedy on Lake Ontario (Whiskey Hill Press, 2006)
Passages on Inland Waters (Whiskey Hill Press, 2004)
The Edge Walker's Guide to Lake Ontario Beach Combing (Whiskey Hill Press, 2002)